D1605513

LOUIS VUITTON CUP
CHALLENGER RACES FOR THE AMERICA'S CUP

America's Cup® '95

THE CITIZEN CUP
DEFENDER RACES FOR THE AMERICA'S CUP

AMERICA'S CUP '95

THE OFFICIAL RECORD

THE LOUIS VUITTON CUP
THE CITIZEN CUP
THE AMERICA'S CUP

AUTHOR:
Bill Center

FEATURED PHOTOGRAPHERS:
Bob Grieser
Sally Samins
Kaoru Soehata

AMERICA'S CUP '95 SPONSORS:
Port of San Diego • Citizen • ESPN • Bayliner

AMERICA'S CUP '95 SUPPLIERS:
Aqua Quorum • Helly Hansen • Hewlett Packard • Moët & Chandon
Motorola • Mount Gay • Trimble • Vuarnet • Yachting

CORPORATE SUPPORT FOR THE OFFICIAL RECORD *PROVIDED BY:*

TEHABI BOOKS
DEL MAR, CALIFORNIA

America's Cup '95: The Official Record has been published in cooperation with the organizing committee of the 1995 America's Cup. It is the exclusive official record of this event and bears the official marks of the America's Cup under the permission of America's Cup Properties, Inc. and the San Diego Yacht Club.

America's Cup '95: The Official Record was conceived and produced by Tehabi Books, Del Mar, California. Nancy Cash–*Managing Editor;* Sam Lewis–*Project Art Director;* Andy Lewis–*Art Director;* Tom Lewis–*Editorial and Design Director;* Sharon Lewis–*Controller;* Chris Capen–*President.*

America's Cup '95: The Official Record was written by Bill Center. Additional support was also provided by Jay Posner–*Copy Editor;* Laura Georgakakos–*Copy Editor* and Kathi George–*Copy Proofer.*

Copyright © 1995 by Tehabi Books, Inc.

All rights reserved. No part of this publication may be used or reproduced in any manner whatsoever without written permission from the publisher except in the case of brief quotations embodied in critical articles and reviews. No use of the America's Cup image or logo is permitted.

For additional copies of this book, corporate customized editions or for more information please contact: Chris Capen, Tehabi Books, 13070 Via Grimaldi, Del Mar, California, 92014, USA (619)481-7600.

Tehabi Books, in association with The Basic Foundation, a not-for-profit organization whose primary mission is reforestation, will facilitate the planting of two trees for every one tree used in the manufacture of this book.

Library of Congress Cataloging-in-Publication Data
Center, Bill.
    America's Cup '95: the official record, the Louis Vuitton Cup, the Citizen Cup, the America's Cup / author, Bill Center : featured photographers, Bob Grieser, Sally Samins, Kaoru Soehata.
        p.   cm. —
    ISBN 1-887656-02-2 (hc)
    1. America's Cup races—History.   2. America's Cup races—Records.   3. America's Cup races—Pictorial works.
4. Yach racing—History.   5. Yacht racing—Pictorial works.   I. Title.
GV829.C37 1995
797.1'4—dc20   95-35637
                                                                          CIP

95 96 97 98 99 TBI 10 9 8 7 6 5 4 3 2 1

This edition is printed on acid-free paper that meets the American National Standards Institute Z39.48 Standard.

Printed in Hong Kong through Mandarin Offset.

AMERICA'S CUP '95

THE OFFICIAL RECORD

For eight years, the San Diego Yacht Club has been honored to serve as the Trustee of the America's Cup. During this time, we have seen a number of very exciting and positive changes to the event that have propelled the America's Cup to the forefront of international sporting competitions.

Among many things, we have seen the introduction of the International America's Cup Class (IACC) Boat and the establishment of a Trustees' Committee and protocol to govern the event. We have attracted a worldwide television audience of over 200 million people and the level of international corporate support for the event is stronger than ever.

As the Cup now settles into its proud new home, there are many individuals who deserve our most sincere thanks for the tremendous commitment they have made to the event—from Malin Burnham and Dennis Conner, whose dream first brought the America's Cup to San Diego, to the ceaseless efforts of the defense syndicates that worked to keep the Cup here, to each and every one of the hundreds of volunteers, staff members, sponsors, and supporters who dedicated thousands of hours and literally poured themselves, body and soul, into the America's Cup. It is this intense level of personal dedication that has made the America's Cup the unique event that it is today.

During its stewardship, the San Diego Yacht Club has made important contributions to the general health and stability of the Cup, and we are pleased to be able to say that the future of the America's Cup is extremely bright.

Our warmest congratulations to Team New Zealand and the Royal New Zealand Yacht Squadron. Their victorious effort and the tremendous response of the entire country of New Zealand has demonstrated what this event is all about.

See you in Auckland!

Mike Morton
COMMODORE
San Diego Yacht Club

Frank L. Hope
CHAIRMAN
America's Cup '95

Charles L. Nichols
PRESIDENT
America's Cup '95

OF MAN, BOATS, & NATIONS

AN AMERICA'S CUP HISTORY

As the oldest international sporting trophy in continuous competition, the America's Cup transcends the sport it represents.

Standing 27 inches high and weighing only 134 ounces, few ever have referred to the America's Cup as a work of art. But the beauty of the America's Cup is not in what it is—rather in what it represents.

It reaches far beyond sailing.

The America's Cup is the ultimate symbol of excellence—a prize that celebrates national achievement on an international level.

The America's Cup is not a simple race conducted on a given afternoon. It is a test—a challenge. America's Cup campaigns examine the mettle of nations and man's insatiable desire to succeed. Intelligence, courage, physi-cal skill, technology, and resolve all play a role. Fall short in one area and you fall short in all.

Wrap this in a history that is unmatched by any other sport-ing endeavor and you have a unique international event—an event whose 144-year history must be understood in order to be appreciated.

America: 1851

On May 1, 1851, a New York newspaper reported that "Mr. W. H. Brown, foot of Twelfth Street, has finished his yacht for the World's Fair, and will test on Friday her powers of sailing in a match with Mr. Stevens's yacht *Maria*."

Mr. Brown's yacht was *America*, which would

become the most famous yacht in history. Later that year, *America* would score the United States' first victory in an international sporting competition. Soon, she would supply the impetus and lend her name to the international sailing competition that became known as the America's Cup.

On that same May day in 1851, the International Exhibition, or "World's Fair," opened in London. The Exhibition was to be a celebration of progress in the arts, sciences, and industry. The plan was to send *America* to England to take part in the festivities and to be an example of Yankee shipbuilding. Providing an example of Yankee shipbuilding wasn't all of it, however. *America's* owners, including John Cox Stevens, owner of the aforementioned *Maria*, hoped to win wagers with her.

America was designed by George Steers, who also supervised her construction. She was shaped along the lines of the Sandy Hook pilot boat. These were typically fast craft, designed to lead ships safely into port. *America* was a schooner, with her two masts raked sharply aft. She was about 95 feet long on deck, with a bowsprit projecting out 17 feet. She drew 11 feet and had a relatively narrow beam of about 23 feet. Distinguishing features were her very fine, concave bow, low freeboard, and simple sailplan.

On June 21, 1851, *America* sailed for France, the first yacht to cross the Atlantic in either direction. After being provisioned, *America* sailed for the town of Cowes on the Isle of Wight, the home of the Royal Yacht Squadron, which had been formed in 1815. By 1851, yachting had a 250-year tradition in England. Yachting in America dated back only about seven years to 1844, when the New York Yacht Club (NYYC) was formed aboard *Gimcrack*, another John Cox Stevens yacht.

Stevens issued a friendly challenge to "any and all schooners of the Old World" for a race. The challenge was ignored by the British, but as *America* waited for a race, Stevens had the good sense to enter a free-for-all for the Hundred Guinea Cup. That race, "open to yachts belonging to clubs of all nations," was to be clockwise around the Isle of Wight. In addition to the 100-guinea cash prize (a guinea was worth slightly more than a pound), there was a silver trophy.

On August 22, 1851, *America* sailed against fifteen English cutters and schooners, ranging in size from the 47-ton cutter *Aurora* to the 392-ton *Brilliant*. *America* was in the middle at approximately 170 tons. In keeping with the custom of the day, the race started with the yachts anchored. *America* overran her anchor and was the last to start. Nevertheless, *America* went on to win by eight minutes over *Aurora*, and her victory became the stuff of legend, at home and abroad. The London Merchant wrote pes-

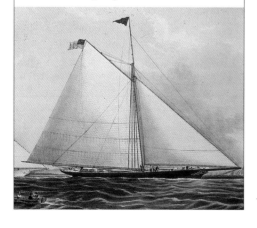

John Cox Stevens's yacht Maria *(below)* had the distinction of beating America *in a set of trials off New York just before the famous schooner set sail for England in 1851. But* Maria *was designed to sail in flat water and was unsuitable for ocean voyages. So it was* America *that crossed the Atlantic and defeated a fleet of 15 English cutters and schooners in the famous race around the Isle of Wight.*

simistically that this win foretold a change in the world's order: "... The empire of the seas must before long be ceded to America ... America, as mistress of the ocean, must overstride the civilized world."

The syndicate returned to America without the boat, but with an ornate if decidedly ugly silver urn. The Royal Yacht Squadron's Hundred Guinea Cup was passed around to the members of the America syndicate. On July 8, 1857, the surviving members of the group gave the trophy to the NYYC, calling it the "America's Cup."

The syndicate drafted a simple Deed of Gift to govern the contest in the future. The 1857 Deed promised: "Any organized yacht club of any foreign country shall always be entitled through any one or more of its members, to claim the right of sailing a match for this cup ... The parties desiring to sail for the Cup may make any match with the yacht club in possession of the same that may be determined upon mutual consent ... The challenging party [is] being bound to give six months' notice in writing, fixing the day they wish to start. This notice to embrace the length, custom-house measurement, rig and name of the vessel." The Deed also said that the match should be "a friendly competition between foreign nations," and that the challenger had to travel to the competition "on its own bottom."

On July 21, 1857, the NYYC sent out invitations to yacht clubs around the world, promising a "spirited contest for the championship." The club also promised a "liberal, hearty welcome and the strictest of fair play."

Spirited the America's Cup usually has been. The issue of "fair play" is far more complex, however. Disputes over "fairness" have been a recurring problem throughout the history of the America's Cup and have received much attention in recent years.

INITIAL DEFENSES: 1870-1887

1870—The first challenge was offered by James Ashbury, from England, for a match in 1869. The NYYC pointed out that clubs, not individuals, could challenge for the Cup, so Ashbury challenged under the auspices of the Royal Thames Yacht Club. Ashbury and the NYYC then tussled over the definition of the word "match" in the Deed of Gift. The word notwithstanding, the NYYC felt strongly that a challenger should face the same conditions as *America* had in 1851, in other words, a fleet race. Ashbury argued that a match meant one-on-one. On this point Ashbury was defeated.

The match actually was sailed on August 8, 1870. Ashbury's yacht, *Cambria*, 108 feet overall, was met with seventeen boats from the NYYC. *Magic*, a small centerboarder of 84 feet overall, won the race. *Cambria* finished eighth, 42 minutes behind the winner. When

A deck scene from Cambria, *the first challenger for the America's Cup in 1870.* Cambria *was owned by James Ashbury, whose two challenges were marred by the first America's Cup controversy. In its first defense, New York Yacht Club turned* Cambria *away with a fleet of 17 defenders.* Cambria *finished tenth. Ashbury's second challenge led to the tradition of one-on-one matches.*

the time allowance was figured (the America's Cup was sailed with a time allowance until 1930 and the J-Class era), *Cambria* dropped to tenth.

1871—Ashbury challenged again with *Livonia*. Again he objected to having to race a fleet. The NYYC refused to consider the change. Ashbury then countered cleverly: He would get a number of yacht clubs in England to challenge for the Cup; each would name his *Livonia* as the challenger. Then he would have the right to race the NYYC fleet 10 or even 20 times.

To settle the one-boat-against-a-fleet issue, the NYYC turned to George Schuyler, the sole surviving member of the America syndicate, for an opinion. Schuyler minced no words: "It seems to me that the present ruling of the club renders the *America's* trophy useless as a Challenge Cup; and that for all sporting purposes it might as well be laid aside as a family plate. . . . " In a letter published in 1871 in the *Spirit of the Times*, Schuyler wrote, "A match means one party contending with another party upon equal terms. . . . "

The ensuing series was one of total confusion. The NYYC still used two boats — *Columbia* and *Sappho* — in its successful defense. By Ashbury's accounting, *Livonia* won. When it was all over, amid misunderstandings and disagreement on the accounting of race scores, Ashbury left without the America's Cup. Upon reaching England, he accused the NYYC of "unfair and unsportsmanlike proceedings," and in his letter to the club he complained that racing in America was not conducted on the same high moral plane that existed in England.

1876—A challenge came from the Royal Canadian Yacht Club in Toronto. The prime mover in the syndicate was Alexander Cuthbert, a Canadian boatbuilder and yacht designer. The New Yorkers were overjoyed. To accommodate the yacht they waived the Deed's requirement of six months' notice so that the contest could be held that very year.

Perhaps the most salutary thing to come out of this challenge was that when the challenger asked that the match be between one defender and one challenger, the NYYC, in a compromising mood, approved the change. The challenger was *Countess of Dufferin*. At 107 feet overall, she was designed, built, and skippered by Cuthbert. She was the first challenger to sail with a centerboard.

This was the first America's Cup to start with the boats not at anchor; the start was timed, as it is today. The unfinished Canadian yacht lost two races to the defender, *Madeleine*, by 19 minutes on average.

Although there were 17 defenders pitted against the challenger Cambria *in the first America's Cup defense of 1870, the "small," 84-foot centerboarder* Magic *(below) won the race. Centerboarders gave the New York Yacht Club a huge advantage in the earliest defenses since James Ashbury's challengers had to sail across the Atlantic, requiring the use of a keel.*

The Countess of Dufferin *(opposite) was the first Canadian yacht to challenge for the America's Cup, in 1876. She was also the last schooner to race for the America's Cup. Owned by designer and boatbuilder Alexander Cuthbert, the* Countess of Dufferin *was the first challenger under the new one challenger/one defender rule.*

1881—Cuthbert returned with the 70-foot *Atalanta*, the first sloop to challenge. The American defender was *Mischief*, only the second metal yacht constructed in America. *Atalanta* lost to *Mischief* by 33 minutes on average.

1885—The first Royal Yacht Squadron challenge. Sir Richard Sutton's *Genesta* sailed against *Puritan*, the first America's Cup design from Edward Burgess, of Boston. The fifth defense, between *Puritan* and *Genesta*, is considered the high-water mark in international sportsmanship in this particular arena. Before the start of the 1885 match, *Puritan*, the defender, on port tack, tried to cross *Genesta*, on starboard tack. The foul carried away *Genesta's* bowsprit. Because a boat on starboard has the right of way over a boat on port, the committee ruled *Puritan* out of the race. Informed by the race committee that all he need do was sail the race for the victory, Sir Richard declined. "We are very much obliged for the honor, but we came to race the Cup defender and cannot accept a walk-over." Sir Richard lost, 2-0.

1887—A challenge is issued from James Bell of the Royal Clyde Yacht Club in Scotland. His challenging yacht, *Thistle*, designed by George Watson, was defeated by NYYC's *Volunteer*.

The Great Sloops: 1893-1920

1893—If Sir Richard Sutton's challenge from the Royal Yacht Squadron was a high-water mark, the challenges of Windham Thomas Wyndam-Quin, the fourth Earl of Dunraven, from that same club were nadirs. Dunraven challenged first in 1889, but the details couldn't be agreed upon. In 1892 he tried again, naming *Valkyrie II* as his challenger. The races were held in 1893.

Dunraven's *Valkyrie II* lost to *Vigilant*, a Nathanael Herreshoff design—the first of his record five America's Cup defenders. *Vigilant* signaled the end of wholesome boats in the America's Cup. What followed were a series of boats described as "the great sloops," or less affectionately as "rule-cheaters" or "freaks." These one-masted sloops showed huge overhangs, which increased their waterline length, and thus their speed, when they heeled over.

1895—Dunraven returned with *Valkyrie III*. An estimated 65,000 people watched the 1895 America's Cup off New York—most of them on hired spectator boats. In the second race, after a near-collision, *Valkyrie* luffed, turning away from *Defender* into the wind. This action caused her main boom to foul *Defender's* starboard topmost shroud, which popped from the spreader. The NYYC rightfully disqualified *Valkyrie*, but Dunraven argued, in spite of the evidence, that his boat hadn't fallen off. He refused an

*A*talanta *was the first sloop to challenge for the America's Cup, in 1881. Although* Atalanta *lost by an average margin of 33 minutes, Cuthbert wanted his second challenger to race again for the trophy the following year. New York Yacht Club drove off the bid by making a rule that the same vessel couldn't sail in two straight America's Cups.*

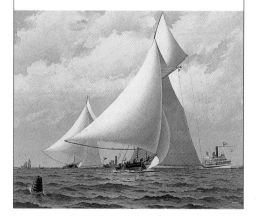

offer by syndicate head Oliver Iselin to resail the race, saying this would be an admission that he was guilty.

Dunraven published in the *London Field* an article in which he accused the NYYC of fraud. The NYYC was not wrong or at fault in this particular matter; still the bitterness and embarrassment of the "Dunraven Affair" nearly killed off the America's Cup.

1899—Following Dunraven, the America's Cup was in desperate need of a savior. The NYYC found its man in a challenge from the greatest diplomat the event has ever known—Sir Thomas Lipton. As a child, Lipton had lived in America, supporting himself by working odd jobs. At 19, he returned to Scotland and opened a grocery store that grew into a world-wide food and tea empire by the time he was 50.

Through 1930, Lipton would launch five challenges. All lost. But all five were sailed in a spirit of sportsmanship missing from many previous America's Cup campaigns. In 1899, Lipton's *Shamrock* lost all three races by decisive margins to *Columbia*, a Herreshoff design considered one of the most beautiful boats ever built.

1901—For the first time in America's Cup history, a scale model was tank tested before the boat was built. The idea was that of Lipton and designer George Watson, who was working on his fourth challenger. Lipton's *Shamrock* was fast, but his team was no match for skipper Charles Barr's crew on *Columbia*, which swept the series.

1903—Encouraged by the relatively equal boat speeds in the 1901 match, Lipton hurried back for his third challenge in five years. This time, it was no contest. A syndicate of New York millionaires, led by William Rockefeller and Cornelius Vanderbilt, gave Herreshoff an unlimited budget. He developed *Reliance*, at 144-feet and 16,000-square feet of sail, the largest boat ever to compete in the America's Cup. *Reliance* swept all three races.

1920—Lipton's fourth challenge, in 1907, was rejected when he suggested that the Cup be sailed in smaller yachts of about 110 feet overall and 75 feet on the water. In 1914, Lipton challenged yet again, once more suggesting the competition be held in smaller boats. The NYYC said, in essence, that challengers didn't write the rules, the defender did. Yet, when Lipton backed down and challenged without conditions, the club, apparently satisfied that it had proven it was in control, accepted his original terms. The match would be sailed in 75-footers, but the challenge never took place because World War I broke out that same year.

The America's Cup is a game of famous men as well as great yachts. Two of the legends were Sir Thomas Lipton and Nathanael Herreshoff. The grocery baron Lipton (above) entered the America's Cup when it was mired in one of its greatest controversies. Between 1899 and 1930, Lipton challenged five times. All lost. But Lipton brought the element of sportsmanship to the event. Herreshoff (below) designed a record six successful defenders between 1893 and 1920.

Defender *was the second design* of Nathanael Herreshoff *to successfully defend the* America's Cup, *in 1895.* Defender *sailed during the era of the "great sloops," which were renowned for their huge sailplans and long overhangs. Losing chal-* lenger Lord Dunraven *charged the crew of* Defender *had cheated his* Valkyrie III *by adding weight to increase the sloop's waterline length.* Valkyrie III *was also disqualified in one race for fouling* Defender *in a near collision.*

Nevertheless, Lipton's *Shamrock IV* remained in New York and waited for a match that finally took place six years later. *Shamrock IV* won the first race, although the American defender, *Resolute*, suffered a breakdown and did not finish. This was one of the few times a defender has broken down in a Cup match, and the only time the defender hasn't finished a race. *Shamrock IV* certainly was competitive, so Lipton announced he would keep the boat in New York and challenge for the next year, 1921. The New Yorkers rejected the challenge, saying it didn't conform to the Deed of Gift.

J-Class Boats: 1930-1937

1930—The J-Class sloops had a brief but beautiful run in the America's Cup. They sailed from 1930 to 1937 and during that span, only 10 of the gracious sloops were built. The J's were a victim of timing. The first four J's were built in 1929, the year of the Wall Street crash. The era ended with the start of World War II.

The elderly Lipton returned one more time for the first defense to be sailed in J's. The class was not the only innovation for 1930. This was the New York Yacht Club's first defense sailed in Newport, Rhode Island. Lipton's *Shamrock V* was beaten by the Harold Vanderbilt-skippered *Enterprise*, which was designed by Starling Burgess, the son of famed designer Edward Burgess.

1934—After the death of Lipton, T.O.M. Sopwith challenged for England. For the 1934 match, the NYYC initiated a rule that all boats must have identical ratings. The rule ended the practice of time allowances and established the head-to-head match racing still used today.

Sopwith's *Endeavour* came as close to winning the America's Cup as any challenger before 1983. *Endeavour* won the first two races in the best-of-seven series against *Rainbow*, was leading the third race by 6 1/2 minutes before it made a tactical error, and almost won the fourth race on a protest. *Rainbow* won four straight races to successfully defend. The restored *Endeavour* was in San Diego throughout the 1995 America's Cup.

1937—After the 1934 defense, Vanderbilt helped author the International Yacht Racing rules, which are used in the America's Cup and most sailboat races to this day. The J era ended with the best of the breed, *Ranger*, defeating Sopwith's *Endeavour II*.

12-Meter Era: 1958-1987

1958—After a 20-year hiatus, due in part to World War II, NYYC Commodore

After the 1903 match, Lipton sought to challenge in a class smaller than the great sloops. He sought a 75-foot waterline limit. At first, the New York Yacht Club balked. Finally, a challenge was accepted for 1914. But the start of World War I scrubbed the match. Lipton kept the boat, Shamrock IV *(below), in New York and the match was sailed in 1920. Lipton won a race against* Resolute *and attempted to challenge again with* Shamrock IV *in 1921. The New York Yacht Club rejected the bid.*

Henry Sears went to England in 1956 to discuss with Sir Ralph Gore, commodore of the Royal Yacht Squadron, whether there was interest in continuing America's Cup racing in boats much smaller than J-Class yachts. This resulted in the 12-Meter era.

Two rule changes were significant. The Deed of Gift was amended to read, "The competing yachts or vessels, if one mast, shall be not less than forty-four feet nor more than ninety feet on the load waterline." (Forty-four feet corresponded to the minimum waterline length of a 12-Meter.) The requirement that a challenger sail to the competition on its own bottom also was waived.

The first post-war challenge was between the defender, *Columbia,* and the challenger, *Sceptre,* from the Royal Yacht Squadron. *Columbia,* designed by Olin J. Stephens II, won easily.

1962—Defender *Weatherly* defeated the Alan Payne-designed Australian challenger *Gretel.* After learning that Payne tested models in New Jersey and used American products, in particular sailcloth from the great American sailmaker Ted Hood, the NYYC forbade the use of American testing facilities and products for challengers. They accomplished this through an interpretation of the Deed of Gift, applying a "country-of-origin" test on the design of a yacht, its designer, and its equipment. *America,* you will recall, had been "an example of Yankee ship-building," and this change returned the competition to its roots: The America's Cup would again be a test of a nation's technology and industry, as well as its sailors.

1964—Immediately after the 1962 defense, the NYYC issued a memorandum saying that in the event it successfully defended the Cup in 1964—which it easily did with *Constellation's* sweep of *Sovereign*—it would regard all challenges received within 30 days after the last race as arriving simultaneously. It would then determine which to accept.

The club also made it clear that it expected to defend the Cup in 12-Meter yachts and that it believed that "It would be in the best interest of the sport and of the competition for the America's Cup if such matches were not held more frequently than once every three years."

Before 1962, a challenger would challenge, and the NYYC would respond. Challengers could work on their designs for years, and New York had only 10 months or less to meet them. Now New York was establishing the timing, and controlling the type of yacht to be used.

If New York took something significant away from the challengers in 1962, it gave

*T*he Great Depression ironically paralleled one of the greatest chapters in America's Cup history. The elegant J-Class sloops graced the three defenses of the '30s. Enterprise *(above) defeated* Shamrock V *in the last bid by Sir Thomas Lipton, in 1930.* Endeavour *(below) won the first two races of the 1934 match before* Rainbow *rallied to win four straight races. World War II spelled the end of the costly J's.*

them what would turn out to be the greatest gift of all: multiple challenges.

1967—Within three days of the conclusion of the 1967 match, in which the great *Intrepid* beat the Australian *Dame Pattie*, the NYYC received bids from several challengers, all of whom agreed to an elimination series of races in 1970. The winner then earned the right to challenge the NYYC for the Cup. Such intramural competition was an edge the defenders had enjoyed since the earliest days of the America's Cup.

1970—*Gretel II* defeated Baron Marcel Bich's *France* in the first multinational challenge, but lost to the modified *Intrepid* in one of the closest series ever.

1974—Australian businessman Alan Bond made his first America's Cup appearance, defeating the French for the right to challenge. On the American side, the new aluminum 12-Meter *Courageous* faced serious opposition from the remodified *Intrepid*, which was being skippered by San Diego's Gerry Driscoll. At the last moment, another San Diegan, Dennis Conner, was brought aboard *Courageous* to help skipper Bob Bavier with the starts and tactics. *Courageous* won the right to defend, then defeated *Southern Cross*.

1977—Replaced by Conner as skipper of *Mariner* during the 1974 trials, Ted Turner returned as skipper of *Courageous*, won the right to defend, and then routed Bond's *Australia*.

1980—For the first time, Conner was skippering a boat in the America's Cup. And for the first time, there were more challengers than defense candidates. Conner's *Freedom* easily defeated Bond's *Australia* in five races. But the stage was set for 1983.

1983—After 132 years, the New York Yacht Club finally lost the Cup. There were seven challengers from five nations. The best was designed by Ben Lexcen for Alan Bond. The boat was the wing-keeled *Australia II*.

Australia II was skippered by John Bertrand, a sailmaker who ran the North Sails loft in Melbourne, Australia. *Liberty*, the American defender, was a conventional 12-Meter skippered by Conner.

Conner won the first two races, although *Australia II* broke down in the second race. In the third race, the Australians won by 3:14—then a record margin for a challenger. Conner sailed the fourth race perfectly, including port-tacking *Australia II* at the start, and won by a razor-thin 43 seconds. The score was 3-1, but then *Australia* won the next two races, making the score 3-3.

On September 26, 1983, Bertrand skippered *Australia II* to victory in the decisive seventh race. The longest winning streak in history had ended. The America's Cup was Australia's cup.

In 1970, Australia's Gretel II *(below) defeated Baron Marcel Bich's* France *in the Cup's first multinational challenge.* Gretel II *then lost a close match to the remodeled* Intrepid, *which became the first boat since* Columbia *in 1899 and 1901 to successfully defend the America's Cup twice.*

1987—The only defense in Australia proved what 1983 indicated. Multiple challenges had tipped the scales against the defenders. In '83, there were seven challengers from five nations against three defenders. In Australia, there were 15 challengers from six nations against four defenders.

The Louis Vuitton Cup challenger finals came down to a match of Conner's *Stars & Stripes* against the Chris Dickson-skippered *Kiwi Magic*, representing New Zealand's first America's Cup bid.

Stars & Stripes won the hotly contested challenger finals 4-1, then defeated Royal Perth Yacht Club's defender, *Kookaburra III*, skippered by designer Iain Murray, by 4-0 in the America's Cup.

For the second time in less than four years, the America's Cup was moving to a new home—this time, the San Diego Yacht Club (SDYC).

THE CATAMARAN AND THE 90-FOOTER: 1988

Conner's victory in Australia took both the winning team and New Zealand's Michael Fay by surprise.

A merchant banker in Auckland, Fay expected New Zealand to win the America's Cup after *Kiwi Magic* posted a 37-1 record through the semifinals of the Louis Vuitton Cup. Fay was stunned by the loss to *Stars & Stripes* in the challenger finals.

As for the winners, neither Conner's team nor the SDYC knew what to do with their prize. As the winners discussed when and where to hold their first defense, Fay launched a preemptive strike.

Fay instructed his lawyer to read the Deed of Gift carefully. The lawyer, Andrew Johns, noted that the Deed still allowed challengers to sail in single-masted boats up to 90 feet on the waterline, as noted in the 1956 Deed amendment. He also noted that the SDYC didn't have a plan to accept all challenges as being simultaneous.

On July 17, 1987, Fay gave the SDYC 10 months' notice of his intention to challenge in a boat 90 feet on the water. The boat he proposed was on the edge of technology. Race boats of this size—Fay's boat ultimately was more than 130 feet overall—hadn't been built since 1937 and the J-Class era. In one fell swoop, Fay took the prerogative away from the Cup-holder. Fay would dictate the size of the boat as well as the timing of the event. It was, unquestionably, a sneak attack, but also completely legal.

The wing-keeled Australia II *(above) was the boat that ended New York Yacht Club's 132-year hold on the America's Cup in 1983. Skippered by John Bertrand,* Australia II *rallied from a 3-1 deficit, concluding its 4-3 victory over Dennis Conner's* Liberty *on September 26, 1983.*

In 1987, off Fremantle, Western Australia, Dennis Conner's Stars & Stripes *(opposite) became the first American challenger to win the America's Cup. After losing the Cup with* Liberty, *Conner formed his own challenge out of the San Diego Yacht Club and developed the powerful* Stars & Stripes *('87) to match Australia's wicked combination of strong winds and steep seas.* Stars & Stripes *routed defender* Kookaburra III *4-0.*

At first, the SDYC tried to negotiate with Fay for a multinational challenge in mutually agreed upon boats. When that failed, SDYC announced in November of 1987 that it would defend the America's Cup with a catamaran.

San Diego commenced building two 60-foot catamarans, one with a solid wing sail, the other with a standard "soft" sailplan. San Diego conducted its own study of the Deed, done by Ed du Moulin and Harmon Hawkins, and concluded the catamaran was legal under the Deed of Gift, certainly as legal as Fay's 90-footer.

On September 7 and 9, 1988, Fay's huge monohull, *New Zealand*, met the wing-sail *Stars & Stripes* ('88). The catamaran won both races easily.

New Zealand's Sir Michael Fay caught the San Diego Yacht Club off guard with his "Big Boat Challenge" of 1988. Measuring 134 feet in overall length, New Zealand *(below) was designed to catch the first-time defenders in a one-on-one battle against a boat they were unable to match. Instead of trying to duplicate* New Zealand, *the SDYC decided to defend with a catamaran.*

Fay immediately filed suit in the New York Supreme Court, which had final jurisdiction over the Deed of Gift. Fay argued that a catamaran versus a monohull was an unfair "match," as that word was intended in the Deed of Gift; and that the defender was bound to compete on equal terms in a "like or similar boat."

San Diego argued that the only design limitation in the Deed of Gift was that the competing vessel must be "propelled by sails only . . . (and) if of one mast, shall be less than forty-four nor more than ninety feet on the load water-line." Its catamaran fitted comfortably within those two dimensions.

The original ruling favored New Zealand. In ruling for Fay, Judge Carmen Ciparick stated, " . . . The conclusion is inescapable that the donor contemplated the defending vessel to relate in some way to the specifications of the challenger." Also persuasive were the following lines in the Deed: "This Cup is donated upon the condition that it shall be preserved as a perpetual Challenge Cup for friendly competition between foreign countries." The judge determined that "the emphasis of the America's Cup is on competition and sportsmanship. The intentions of the donors were to foster racing between yachts or vessels on somewhat competitive terms. . . ."

On March 28, 1989, Judge Ciparick awarded the America's Cup to the Mercury Bay Boating Club in New Zealand. The San Diego Yacht Club immediately appealed.

In September, the Appellate Division reversed Judge Ciparick's decision, writing: "In finding that the vessels must be 'somewhat evenly matched,' the court promulgated a rule that is neither expressed in, nor inferable from, the language of the Deed. . . ."

Fay appealed. And on April 26, 1990, the State of New York Court of Appeals concluded that nowhere in the Deed of Gift had the donors expressed an intention to prohibit the use of multihull vessels or to require the defender of the Cup to race a vessel of the same type as the vessel to be used by the challenger. The court also

*P*erhaps the most controversial boat ever to sail for the America's Cup, Dennis Conner's high-tech, wing-sail Stars & Stripes catamaran easily routed New Zealand's "Big Boat" in the 1988 match off San Diego. The use of the 60-foot catamaran also spawned a series of court battles that eventually ended in a SDYC victory.

rejected Mercury Bay's contention that the phrase "friendly competition between countries" connoted a requirement that the defender race a vessel of the same type or even substantially similar to the challenging vessel.

The court returned the Cup to San Diego.

THE INTERNATIONAL AMERICA'S CUP CLASS: 1992-

As soon as the courts concluded their work, the San Diego Yacht Club established a protocol covering its first defense in 1992. Because San Diego is a region of light winds, the SDYC decided the 12-Meter was not a viable boat for the region so an international group of designers developed the new International America's Cup Class.

The IACC boats were longer and had more sail area than the venerable 12's. They also were lighter and constructed of space-age carbon-fiber composites. The America's Cup went high-tech and high-performance.

There were eight challengers from seven nations—Australia, Italy, France, Spain, Sweden, Japan, and New Zealand. And there were two defense syndicates—Team Dennis Conner and the new America³ program established by Kansas millionaire Bill Koch.

Through the Louis Vuitton Cup challenger semifinals, the Rod Davis-skippered *New Zealand* seemed to have an edge on its rival challengers. But a lingering dispute over the Kiwis' use of their controversial bowsprit wouldn't go away.

Under constant attack from *Il Moro di Venezia* skipper Paul Cayard, the Kiwis cracked. Having just won a race on the water to take an apparent 4-1 lead in the best 5-of-9 challenger finals, New Zealand saw its fourth victory removed from the books when Cayard finally prevailed in the bowsprit protest. *Il Moro* won four straight races to win the trials 5-3.

On the defense side of the equation, Koch's technology-driven program beat off the relentless efforts of Conner's older and slower *Stars & Stripes*.

Most experts believed *Il Moro di Venezia* would take the America's Cup to Italy. But between the end of the defense finals and the America's Cup, Koch's team had been busy replacing the keel on the long-and-narrow breakthrough design known as *America³*.

With Buddy Melges on the wheel, assisted by skipper Koch, *America³* scored a 4-1 victory over the Italians, whose three-second win in race two was the closest ever in an America's Cup match. Over the five-race series, the average time difference between the two boats had been only 47 seconds.

*B*ill Koch celebrated victory (below) after his "technology-driven" America³ program of 1992 resulted in a 4-1 victory over Il Moro di Venezia. Although America³ (opposite) is shown sailing downwind while the Paul Cayard-skippered Italians are still driving toward the weather mark, the series was much closer than it looked, with only one race decided by more than 65 seconds.

The Syndicates

Profiles of the 1995 Challengers & Defenders

In the aftermath of the 1992 America's Cup, defenders and challengers alike took a deep breath and looked forward to 1995 with reservation.

Although the new International America's Cup Class had been an exciting improvement in 1992 over the venerable 12-Meter, the cost of the 28th defense had gone far beyond expectations.

The Italian challenge had built five new boats and spent more than $85 million in its Louis Vuitton Cup-winning bid with *Il Moro di Venezia.* And Bill Koch had spent more than $65 million—mostly from his personal fortune—building four boats for the successful *America³* defense.

All told, eight challengers and two defenders spent in excess of $350 million funding 25 boats for 1992. Immediately following the 1992 event, a cost-cutting committee was formed by the San Diego Yacht Club to look at the America's Cup. The recommendations not only led to some changes for 1995, they opened the door to some major innovations that improved the event.

To cut costs, each syndicate was limited to two new boats and 45 sails for 1995. Spying was eliminated and the course was changed to a windward-leeward track, eliminating the need for reaching sails.

A new sense of cooperation between defenders and challengers grew out of the meetings. The seven challengers and three defenders competing in America's Cup '95 built 14 new boats and spent less than $200 million. The stage also was set for agreements that improved the public's access to the event.

During the IACC World Championship in the fall of 1994, three races were sailed on San Diego Bay where more than 30,000 spectators viewed the boats.

All syndicates opened their gates for three open houses during the round-robins. Then, on April 9, the shrouds came off the keels as defender and challenger semifinalists alike named the boats to be used through the remainder of the Louis Vuitton and Citizen Cups.

Yes, there were hitches and protests. There always are in the America's Cup. But the popularity of the event soared in 1995—thanks in part to the presence of the first women's crew in America's Cup history.

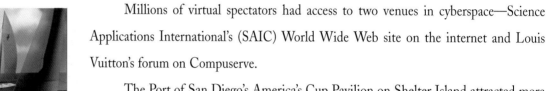

*L*ouis Vuitton Malletier made its strongest presence yet in the 1995 America's Cup. In addition to organizing the Louis Vuitton Cup with the CORC, Louis Vuitton managed the various media centers worldwide. The America's Cup Louis Vuitton Media Centre (below) was located at Shelter Island's Koni Kai Resort. An innovation for 1995 was the computer-produced Virtual Reality coverage (above) using GPS data from the racing boats. The system was made possible by Louis Vuitton and supported by Silicon Graphics, Trimble, C&I, Getris and Medialab.

Millions of virtual spectators had access to two venues in cyberspace—Science Applications International's (SAIC) World Wide Web site on the internet and Louis Vuitton's forum on Compuserve.

The Port of San Diego's America's Cup Pavilion on Shelter Island attracted more than 112,000 visitors in 40 days. And the Louis Vuitton Media Center at the Kona Kai Club Resort on Shelter Island brought over 2,000 international journalists and photographers much closer to the heart of the event than they were in 1992.

As for the fleets, there was one more defense candidate in 1995 than in '92—and one fewer challenger. Fifteen months before the start of the trials, there were 10 challengers from seven nations. But the *Il Moro di Venezia* effort for '95 collapsed in the wake of the death of its director, Raul Gardini. The Challenger of Record Committee eliminated the struggling Russian bid after it missed several deadlines. And the second French challenge, representing the Yacht Club d'Antibes, withdrew just months before the start of the trials even though its yacht, *Harmony*, was almost completed.

That left seven challengers from five nations—two each from New Zealand and Australia and one each from France, Spain, and Japan. Pitted against the challenger fleet were three defenders—the women of America³, the veteran campaigners from Team Dennis Conner, and the first-time bid by PACT 95.

Throughout the trials and actual defense of America's Cup '95, there existed a closer bond between the event and the community than was present during the San Diego Yacht Club's first two defenses. Alas, San Diego's best America's Cup was also its last.

"Years from now, when we look back on San Diego, it will be with warmth," said Team New Zealand skipper Russell Coutts. "Our sport has made friends here."

The April 9 public keel un-veilings of the finalists for the Louis Vuitton and Citizen Cups were one of the highlights of America's Cup '95. By mutual consent, each compound was open to the public for a ceremony that featured the un-shrouding of the boat's keel. Clockwise from upper left: OneAustralia, Mighty Mary, Black Magic, Stars & Stripes, Young America *and* OneAustralia. *Before April 9, only Ken McAlpine's measurement team had seen all the keels.*

TEAM NEW ZEALAND

As it turned out, there was nothing magical to the *Black Magics.* No breakthrough design. No top-secret sails. "We were rock solid," said Peter Blake after Team New Zealand easily swept five straight races off Team Dennis Conner to claim the America's Cup.

"If we had a secret, it was in our attention to every detail through a team approach. The designers, builders, sailmakers, and crew all worked together. There were no superstars on the boat." This was evident from Blake's personal involvement: Away from the America's Cup, Blake is one of the world's top blue-water skippers. On *Black Magic,* he served as caddie for mainsheet trimmer Warwick Fleury.

"The biggest difference between this campaign and our previous efforts were the superstars," said grinder Andrew Taylor, the only man to sail on all four New Zealand America's Cup bids. "We didn't have any. The past campaigns were management or design driven. This time, the direction began from onboard the boat."

There was another difference between this and past New Zealand efforts. This one carried through to the end.

1987—The Chris Dickson-skippered *Kiwi Magic* 12-Meter loses in the challenger finals to Dennis Conner's *Stars & Stripes* after posting a 37-1 record.

1988— The renegade New Zealand "big boat" challenge is buried by Conner's catamaran and the courts.

1992—After building a 4-1 lead before losing a race to the bowsprit protest, New Zealand loses 5-3 to the Paul Cayard-skippered *Il Moro di Venezia* in the challenger finals.

1995—Victory.

Challenger Round-Robins: *Black Magic* is undefeated on the water, losing once when *oneAustralia* successfully protests the Team New Zealand practice of sending Murray Jones to the top of the mast to search for wind. Official count: 22-1.

Louis Vuitton Cup Semifinals: After nine straight wins, *Black Magic* retires early after clinching a berth in the finals.

Louis Vuitton Cup Finals: *Black Magic* defeats *oneAustralia* 5-1, the lone loss being by 15 seconds in a superbly sailed race by both crews.

America's Cup: A 5-0 blitz of Conner's team sailing *Young America. Black Magic* led at all 30 marks and gained on 25 of the 30 legs. Average margin of victory—2:52.

Official record: 41-2. Average margin of victory: 3:06. Percent of 260 legs led: 93. "Pretty awesome," said co-designer Doug Peterson.

BOATS—*Black Magic*

SAIL NOS.—*NZL-32, NZL-38*

CLUB—*Royal New Zealand Yacht Squadron*

SYNDICATE HEAD—*Peter Blake (below left)*

SKIPPER—*Russell Coutts (below right)*

LEAD DESIGNERS—*Doug Peterson and Laurie Davidson*

BUILDER—*McMullen & Wing*

SAILS—*North*

CREW—*Brad Butterworth, Rick Dodson, Tom Schnackenberg, Murray Jones, Warwick Fleury, Simon Daubney, Robbie Naismith, Ross Halcrow, Andrew Taylor, Craig Monk, Jeremy Scantlebury, Matthew Mason, Joe Allen, Dean Phipps, Chris Ward, Tony Rae, Kevin Shoebridge, Mike Spanhake, Mike Quilter, Nick Heron.*

ONEAUSTRALIA

There is a defining date to oneAustralia's challenge—March 5, 1995.

That's when *oneAustralia*—AUS-35—became the first America's Cup contender in the 144-year history of the America's Cup to sink.

"We put up the good fight, but, truthfully, I'd have to say we were handicapped from that day forward . . . that was our best chance that went to the bottom," said skipper John Bertrand, looking back on the formidable *oneAustralia* campaign.

"I don't think you can say enough about the *oneAustralia* effort after their boat sank," said Peter Blake, head of the victorious Team New Zealand challenge. "I doubt we could have done as well had we lost our best boat."

The boat that sank was the key to oneAustralia's challenge—which marked the return to the America's Cup of winning 1983 Australian skipper Bertrand.

AUS-35 was also the boat at the heart of the biggest controversy of America's Cup '95. It was built through a partnership agreement between oneAustralia and Syd Fischer's rival Australian Challenge. Outsiders claimed the agreement violated the rule limiting each team to two new boats. The international jury eventually ruled in oneAustralia's favor.

The first boat Bertrand's team built for the campaign—AUS-31—easily won the 1994 International America's Cup Class World Championship and its long, narrow, and light hull became the prototype for the next generation.

AUS-35 was an extension of AUS-31's lead. Why did AUS-35 sink? The weather conditions were at the upper limits—winds gusting to 20 knots with 5-foot seas and a stiff chop—but not extreme. "We may never know what happened," said Iain Murray, a member of the oneAustralia design team, "other than to say it was a catastrophic failure."

Bertrand's team refused to quit. *OneAustralia* was back on the water in two days with the older AUS-31 hull. Three days after the accident, *oneAustralia* won a key race against NZL-39. After finishing second in the semifinals, the *oneAustralia* crew made major modifications to AUS-31 before the finals.

Alas, it was to no avail. Team New Zealand won the Louis Vuitton Cup finals 5-1. But *oneAustralia* did win one of the best races of the '95 series—Davis and his crew battling to stay in front throughout an 18-mile heat decided by only 15 seconds.

"We got one more win off *Black Magic* than anyone else did," said Bertrand. "I am convinced we were good enough to also take the America's Cup off the defender."

BOATS—*oneAustralia*

SAIL NOS.—*AUS-31, AUS-35*

SYNDICATE HEAD—*John Bertrand (below)*

SKIPPER—*John Bertrand*

HELMSMAN—*Rod Davis*

DESIGNER—*FluidThinking team led by Iain Murray and John Reichel*

BUILDER—*John McConaghy*

SAILS—*North, Sobstad, oneAustralia*

CREW—*Glenn Bourke, Ian Burns, Andrew Cape, Bill Bates, Adam Beashel, Greg Cavill, Iain Smith, Kim Sheridan, Mark Callahan, Nick Moloney, Mark McTeigue, Don McCracken, Mike Mottl, Mark Richards, Matt Shillington, Alan Smith, Paul Westlake.*

TUTUKAKA CHALLENGE

Late in 1994, Chris Dickson pared a quarter off his already austere America's Cup budget . . . then cut that again by a third. Crew members carried their own bedding and linen from New Zealand to San Diego. Cantebury of New Zealand supplied the sailing crew with shirts and shorts so that Dickson's crew would have matching outfits on the boat.

"Instead of cars for each crewman, we've leased two old vans to shuttle people back and forth to the compound," said Dickson, somewhat proudly. "Every penny we have goes into the boat."

No team got more out of its resources. But it wasn't enough.

"I don't think we got everything out of the boat that was there," tactician Peter Lester said after Dickson's challenge was eliminated in the challenger semifinals. "We just ran out of resources."

At the conclusion of his first independent effort, Dickson admitted that his team's budget was under $8 million—or about half that of the next closest budget among the semifinalists.

"It took sacrifice and cooperation from everyone to get here," said Dickson. "We kept cutting expenses until there was no meat left to trim."

The only way Dickson's team made it to San Diego was with the last-minute help of TAG Heuer, which footed the bills. Dickson wanted to name his boat for the Swiss sports watch manufacturer, but agreements between event organizers and each of the syndicates prohibited that idea so Dickson sailed under the generic sail number.

NZL-39 was designed by Bruce Farr, who is 0-for-4 in America's Cup bids. It was the most distinctive boat in the fleet with a sharp, slender bow that made the foredeck team operate like trapeze artists.

Dickson's team was fast out of the gate. NZL-39 lost only one race in the first round-robin and was tied for the second-best record after three rounds.

But on the last—and most important—day of the round-robins, Dickson was over the starting line early against *oneAustralia* and lost a race that eventually doomed NZL-39. That defeat enabled *oneAustralia* to climb into second in the final round-robin standings and have the tiebreaker edge on NZL-39 in the semifinals. That proved decisive.

OneAustralia used the tiebreaker to clinch second in the semifinals before a scheduled, series-ending NZL-39/*oneAustralia* race could be sailed. "It was a sad way to conclude a campaign," said Dickson. "I'd much prefer to race and lose than sit it out."

NZL-39 finished with a 24-12 overall record.

BOAT—NZL-39

SAIL NO.—NZL-39

CLUB—Tutukaka South Pacific Yacht Club

SYNDICATE HEAD—Chris Dickson (below)

SKIPPER—Chris Dickson

DESIGNER—Bruce Farr

BUILDER—Cookson Boats

SAILS—Lidgard

CREW—Peter Lester, Steve Cotton, Jon Bilger, Greg Flynn, Mike Sanderson, Jim Close, Grant Loretz, Kevin Batten, Denis Kendall, David Brooke, Rodney Ardern, Sean Clarkson, Chris Salthouse, Graham Fleury, Kelvin Harrap, Brad Jackson.

NIPPON CHALLENGE

No team worked harder at America's Cup '95 than the Japanese.

The Nippon Challenge was training in San Diego with its first new boat and its 1992 semifinalist a year before the challenger trials began.

Nippon entered two boats in the 1994 IACC World Championship. And in the wake of a disappointing showing, the Japanese completely rebuilt JPN-30, the first new boat they built for '95.

The eight-week project impressed even those rivals who argued that JPN-30A might have violated the new rule limiting each team to two new boats.

BOATS—*Nippon*

SAIL NOS.—*JPN-30, JPN-41*

CLUB—*Nippon Yacht Club*

SYNDICATE HEAD—*Tatsumitsu Yamasaki*

SKIPPER—*Makoto Namba (below)*

HELMSMAN—*John Cutler*

LEAD DESIGNER—*Ichiro Yokoyama*

BUILDER—*Yamaha*

SAILS—*Diamond*

CREW—*Kazuhiko Sofuku, Masahiro Ogawa, Kiyotaka Okabe, Ken Hara, Guy Barron, Kazuyuki Hyodo, Tatsuya Wakinaga, Chris Mason, Hartwell Jordan, Manabu Yoshida, Yasuhiro Yaji, Masami Kimura, Yasuhiro Uchino, Peter Evans.*

"I think everyone will remember how hard the Nippon team worked in 1995," said Makoto Namba, who became one of the event's more popular figures.

Just before the start of the Louis Vuitton Cup trials, syndicate head Tatsumitsu Yamasaki named Namba the skipper of *Nippon*. John Cutler and coach Peter Gilmour had helmed the Japanese entries in the World Championship and Cutler would continue to drive the boat throughout the trials.

But Namba would be skipper.

"Namba may still be learning about the helm," said Cutler. "But he deserves to be the skipper of this boat. He is the bond that brings the crew together—the man most repected by everyone else on the boat."

"Some day, I hope to steer the boat," said Namba. "But right now it is not time for me. I am happy to help where I can."

The Japanese have made incredible gains in their two America's Cups. Although Japan had few big-boat sailors and almost no match racing experience when they issued their first challenge for '92, New Zealand import Chris Dickson drove a mixed *Nippon* crew into the semifinals. *Nippon* again sailed in '95 with a mixed Japanese and English-speaking crew.

The rebuilt JPN-30 had a 9-9 record through the first three round-robins when it was retired in favor of the newer JPN-41—which barely advanced to the semifinals with a 2-4 record in the last round.

Sadly, the semifinals were not kind to the Japanese. Nippon lost all 11 races to finish with an 11-24 overall record.

Concluded Namba: "Our finish was very disappointing. But we must be truthful. We have come a long way . . . and have a long way to go. Japan has learned much in our two challenges."

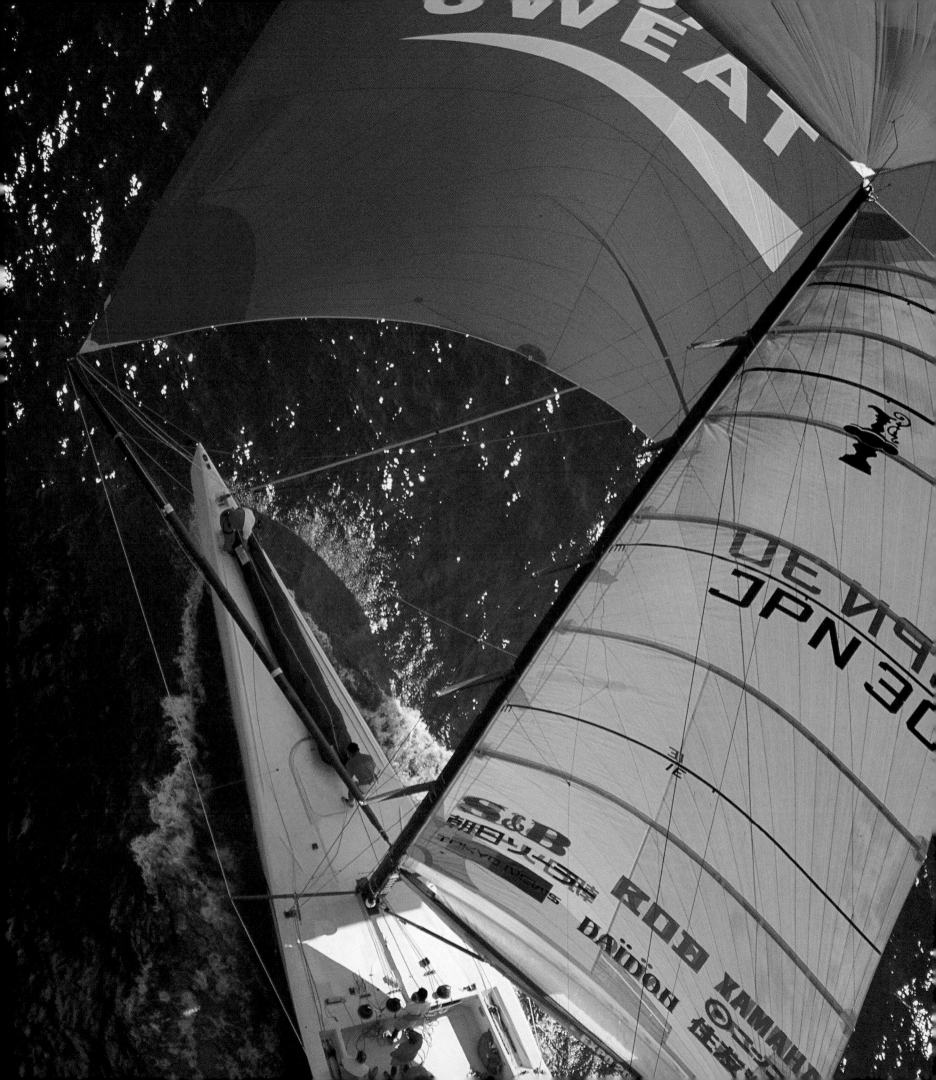

FRANCE AMERICA '95

Marc Pajot had no problems finding the words to describe his third America's Cup challenge.

"Disaster," said the French skipper. "With all the hopes followed by the problems . . . to not make the semifinals, it is a disaster."

Pajot's first two America's Cup challengers—*French Kiss* in Australia in 1987 and *Ville de Paris* in San Diego in 1992—had both reached the Louis Vuitton Cup semifinals. The team's solid performance in '92 raised expectations for '95.

But high hopes quickly became a burden that handicapped the team. France expected to make the semifinals . . . and more . . . in '95. Then came the crash, and the fall.

France's bid began to unravel on December 7, 1994. As *France 2* was being raised from its cradle to be put into the water for the first time in San Diego, the hoist assembly inside the boat broke and the boat fell onto the pavement of its Mission Bay compound. The force of the blow drove the keel blade up through the deck and shattered sections of the hull.

The French team spent almost $1 million and lost a valuable month rebuilding *France 2*. Instead of being ahead of the game, the French were now playing catch-up. And they never regained the lost momentum.

The news kept getting worse. *France 2* was 1-5 in the first round-robin. Pressed into service sooner than expected, the Philippe Briand-designed *France 3* was bidding to break into the top four when the second disaster struck. On February 20, the keel fell off *France 2* as the trial horse was testing a revolutionary new mainsail seven miles west of Mission Bay.

Pajot's troubled team was down to one boat with no test platform. And *France 3* continued to struggle.

At one point, Pajot and tactician Bertrand Pacé turned *France 3* over to François Brenac and Thierry Peponnet. But there was no improvement.

Still, the French entered the last round-robin needing only one more win than *Nippon* to gain the semifinals. But *Nippon* beat *France 3*. Then the French were dismasted while leading *Rioja de España*.

On the final day of the round-robins, *Nippon* rallied to defeat *Rioja de España* by 13 seconds—keeping *France 3* from advancing to the semifinals despite a last-day victory over *Sydney 95*. Pajot's team finished with a 8-16 record.

"Nothing has hurt this bad," said Pajot. "This is a major failure for us. I am in shock because we never expected that we would not make the semifinals."

BOATS—*France 2, France 3*

SAIL NOS.—*FRA-33, FRA-37*

CLUB—*Yacht Club de Sète*

SYNDICATE HEAD—*François Giraudet*

SKIPPER—*Marc Pajot (below)*

DESIGNER—*Philippe Briand*

BUILDER—*Jeanneau/MAG*

SAILS—*North, Elvstrom, Groupe Incidences*

CREW—*Bernard Labro, Jules Mazard, Benoit Briand, Albert Jacobsoone, Xavier Husson, Thierry Chappet, Christian Karcher, Sylvain Barrielle, Jacques Di Russo, Thomas Coville, Fabrice Levet, Yann Gouniot, Laurent Delage, Christian Dumard, Bertrand Pacé, Thierry Peponnet, François Brenac.*

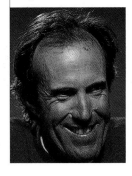

COPA AMERICA '95 DESAFIO ESPAÑOL

For the gritty Spaniards, the 1995 America's Cup was a case of too little, too late.

The last team to arrive in San Diego, skipper Pedro Campos's crew had less than two full practice days on their hurriedly completed *Rioja de España* when the challenger trials began in mid-January.

"We were always behind," said Campos. "We were still testing sails in the races. It was impossible to catch up against the caliber of competition we faced. The more you learn, the faster you move to the next step. But we were always a step or two behind."

BOAT—Rioja de España

SAIL NO.—ESP-42

CLUB—Monte Real Nautico de Yates

SYNDICATE HEAD—Miguel Aguilo

SKIPPER—Pedro Campos (below)

LEAD DESIGNER—Joaquin Coello

BUILDER—Rodman Polyships

SAILS—Diamond

CREW—Francisco Rivero, Jaime Arbones, Miguel Jauregui, Javier Aguado, Agustin Zulueta, Victor Unzueta, Antonio Piris, Javier Arrizabalaga, Inaki Martinez, Marcos Iglesias, Santiago Portillo, Laureano Wizner, Inaki Castaner, Joan Vila, Alejandro Abascal.

"Maybe if we had started much sooner, we could have reached the semifinals. Maybe. But I do know this . . . we were much better than we were in 1992. Our problem was, everyone else was much better, too."

It was the triumphant first-time challenge of 1992—issued to celebrate the 500th anniversary of Christopher Columbus's voyage to America—that encouraged Spain to return in 1995. Three years ago, Spain finished fifth in a fleet of eight challengers.

Money was tighter this time, however, and delayed the construction of the new ESP-42 hull, which was designed by a team led by young naval architect Joaquin Coello. The boat was built in less than two months and shipped directly to San Diego without being tested off Spain.

"Our idea was to gamble on designing the lightest boat possible," said Campos. "Unfortunately for us, almost everyone gambled on boats even lighter than ours. It put us at a disadvantage and we were helpless to change with a one-boat program."

Still, the Spanish put up an admirable fight. Campos's crew of small-boat champions—few of whom had any match racing experience before '92—got everyone's attention with its aggressive prestart maneuvers.

"We have gained much respect from our competitors," tactician Alejandro Abascal said after *Rioja de España* led *Black Magic* for a lap of a round-robin match. "We might lose, but we don't lose without a fight."

After losing 15 straight races, the Spanish beat *Sydney 95* at the end of the third round-robin. In the fourth round-robin, the Spanish again beat *Sydney 95*, won against a dismasted *France 3* and almost knocked *Nippon* out of the semifinals. That 13-second loss to the Japanese proved how far the Spanish had come since the start of the trials. "At the end, I thought we were competitive against all but New Zealand and Australia," said Campos.

Spain had a 3-21 record on the water, but finished ahead of *Sydney 95* in the final scoring.

AUSTRALIAN CHALLENGE

 Although his challenges have had little success, maverick owner Syd Fischer always makes the America's Cup interesting.

In 1983, his *Advance* was so far off the pace in Newport, Rhode Island, that Fischer painted a black nose on the bow and referred to the 12-Meter as "my dog."

In 1987, Fischer's *Steak n' Kidney* might have been the fastest of Australia's three defense candidates. But the boat was eliminated from the trials just as it hit its stride with a new keel.

In 1992, the big swivel-keeled *Challenge Australia* won but one of its 21 races.

Thanks to the controversial cooperative partnership with the oneAustralia challenge, Fischer returned to the America's Cup in '95 with what he considered to be his strongest bid yet. *Sydney 95* was designed by the same consortium that designed oneAustralia's two boats and Fischer's team benefitted from months of testing against the original *oneAustralia* (AUS-31).

SYDNEY 95

Fischer's team got off to a fast start, defeating *France 2* and *Rioja de España* in its first two races to double Fischer's win total of 1992. But trouble was already brewing—in the skies and on the water.

Sydney 95 was the heaviest-air boat in the America's Cup fleet . . . and '95 proved to be a year dominated by light winds. And there were persistent problems in both the depth of the crew (at one point down to one sailing reserve) and the makeup of the afterguard.

Skipper Chris Law was relieved at the end of the first round-robin after having a mid-race dispute with Fischer over modifications made to the boat. For the second round-robin, former on-the-water umpire Neville Wittey handled the starts and tactician Michael Coxon drove the boat during the race. In the third round, former 12-Meter skipper Colin Beashel was flown in from Australia to tandem with Wittey. In the fourth round, Wittey was in charge.

"We spent much of the trials learning what we could do as a team," said Wittey. "We grew as a team and I thought everyone gave it a great effort."

Sydney 95 had its moments . . . especially when the wind came up. *Sydney 95* beat *Nippon*. Fischer's team also twice beat the French. *Sydney 95* compiled a 5-19 record, but finished last in the standings because most of its wins came in the earlier, low-scoring rounds.

After *Sydney 95* was eliminated, Fischer said he wouldn't return for a fifth America's Cup . . . unless either oneAustralia or Team New Zealand won in '95.

BOAT—*Sydney 95*

SAIL NO.—*AUS-29*

SYNDICATE HEAD—*Syd Fischer (below)*

SKIPPER—*Neville Wittey*

DESIGNER—*FluidThinking*

BUILDER—*John McConaghy*

SAILS—*North*

CREW—*Michael Coxon, Syd Fischer, Colin Beashel, David Blanchfield, Tommy Braidwood, Campbell Knox, Andrew Crowe, Greg Kay, Brett Jones, James Mayo, Dom Sudano, Ben Sullivan, Neal McDonald, Andrew Cuddihy, Simon Cunnington, Chris Law.*

TEAM DENNIS CONNER

It rang out daily from loudspeakers in the *Stars & Stripes* compound on San Diego Bay.

More than an anthem, it was a theme. To the beat of the Bee Gees' famous disco tune "Stayin' Alive," Dennis Conner's veteran crew doggedly refused to capitulate during the 1995 defense trials.

"I'm proud of this team," helmsman Paul Cayard said after Team New Zealand scored a 5-0 sweep of Conner's crew—sailing the borrowed *Young America*—in the America's Cup.

"From the earliest days, we knew the score. It was clear that there were major hurdles to overcome. But everyone kept digging in. We wouldn't go away. Even when we were beaten, we refused to lose. If nothing else, we were resilient."

Following his victory in the 1987 America's Cup in Australia, Conner authored a book titled *Comeback.* Even though his 1995 defense bid ultimately ended in decisive defeat, Conner could arguably recycle the *Comeback* logo to chronicle his team's efforts during the defense trials.

BOATS—Stars & Stripes

SAIL NO.—USA-34

SYNDICATE HEAD—Dennis Conner

SKIPPER—Dennis Conner (below left)

HELMSMAN—Paul Cayard (below right)

DESIGN TEAM LEADERS—Bill Trenkle, Chris Todter, Dave Pedrick

BUILDER—Eric Goetz

SAILS—North

CREW—Tom Whidden, Jim Brady, Bill Trenkle, Jud Smith, Brad Rodi, Steve Erickson, Rock Ferrigno, Paul Larkin, Jim Kavle, Jim Nicholas, Josh Belsky, Wally Henry, T. A. McCann, Ralf Steitz, Greg Prussia.

"I think people gave up, counting us out," Conner said. "We always seemed to be on the brink. But they couldn't knock us out."

The storm warnings were posted early. Experts agreed that USA-34 was the slowest of the three new boats designed for the 1995 defense. The situation worsened on March 26 when *Stars & Stripes's* radical new keel almost fell off during a semifinals race. Fearing USA-34 might sink, the crew donned life jackets as pumps were rushed aboard and flotation and marker buoys were hoisted to the top of the mast.

Still, Team Dennis Conner's darkest hours were yet to come. Switching back to the old keel during a rush repair job triggered a rash of protests from rival defenders. The *Stars & Stripes* team was fighting a two-front war—on the water and off—as the days dwindled to a precious few.

The only thing that staved off elimination in the semifinals was a last-minute compromise that sent all three defenders to the finals.

Before the finals, the *Stars & Stripes* crew worked around the clock rebuilding its boat. The USA-34 that was last in the semifinals was first in the finals—saving its best comeback for the final race. Needing a victory to earn the right to defend, *Stars & Stripes* trailed *Mighty Mary* by 4:08 at the last mark—and won by 52 seconds. Amazing? "I have given up trying to explain how we're doing it," said Cayard.

Unfortunately, Conner's team ran out of tricks one step too early. Nothing, not even the borrowed *Young America,* could save them against *Black Magic.*

PACT 95

The seed for the first Maine-based America's Cup effort was planted in 1990 when John Marshall and San Diego's Science Applications International developed the Partnership for America's Cup Technology (PACT) technical program to jump start the 1992 defense in the new International America's Cup Class.

The elements Marshall needed to form the foundation of the PACT 95 syndicate began coming together in early 1993. Fellow Maine resident Kevin Mahaney joined Marshall shortly after winning a silver medal in the Soling Class at the 1992 Olympics. And designer Bruce Nelson also signed up after having worked with Marshall on two Stars & Stripes campaigns and the original PACT project.

Like America's "women's team," PACT 95 had a secondary theme—science and technology, with an emphasis on youth participation. In addition to building a boat and a team, Marshall oversaw the development of a series of public television specials and hands-on programs dedicated to interesting young minds in the technology of the America's Cup.

PACT 95
Partnership for the defense
of the America's Cup

Still, the bottom line was the development of a strong defense contender.

Nelson came up with a solid design in USA-36—*Young America*. But trials of PACT 95 extended beyond the races sailed on the water.

On the night of January 4—nine days before the beginning of the defense trials—tornado-like winds ripped through PACT 95's Mission Bay compound, destroying the team's sail loft and hospitality area. The sail loft was torn off its foundation and thrown against the cradle holding *Young America*. The boat suffered $600,000 in damage, including a series of punctures to the hull. Working around the clock, the team repaired *Young America* in time for the first round of trials.

Nicknamed "Dorothy" following its wild ride, *Young America*—featuring the hull-length mermaid graphic designed by renowned American artist Roy Lichtenstein—had one other brush with disaster. On March 12, while being towed out of Mission Bay for a practice sail, *Young America* hit a rogue, three-meter wave and suffered extensive damage. Again, the crew worked around the clock to make the necessary repairs.

Young America had the best record through the defense round-robins (14-6) and appeared headed toward winning the Citizen Cup with a 7-1 record in the semifinals. But PACT 95 struggled in the finals, losing the right to defend to Team Dennis Conner—although *Young America's* overall won-loss record of 24-12 was easily the best among the three defense candidates. Conner's team then paid PACT 95 the highest compliment by requesting PACT 95's permission to use *Young America* to defend the America's Cup.

BOAT—*Young America*

SAIL NO.—*USA-36*

SYNDICATE HEAD—*John Marshall (below left)*

SKIPPER—*Kevin Mahaney (below right)*

LEAD DESIGNER—*Bruce Nelson*

BUILDER—*Eric Goetz*

SAILS—*North*

CREW—*John Kostecki, Bruce Nelson, Robert Hopkins, Ken Read, Andreas Josenhans, Moose McClintock, Grant Spanhake, Steve Calder, Roy Disney, Stuart Felker, Hal Sears, Matt Welling, Matt Smith, Michael Herlihy, Joseph Fordney, Stewart Silvestri, Bruce Epke, Gordie Shaver, Gordon Wagner.*

AMERICA³

AMERICA³.
The Women's Team

BOATS—America³, Mighty Mary

SAIL NOS.—USA-23, USA-43

SYNDICATE HEAD—Bill Koch (below left)

SKIPPER—Leslie Egnot (below right)

DESIGN TEAM LEADERS—Vincent Moeyersoms,

Dr. Jerry Milgram, Dr. Heiner Meldner

BUILDER—Eric Goetz

SAILS—Sobstad

CREW—Dawn Riley, Dave Dellenbaugh,

Courtenay Becker-Dey, Melissa Purdy,

Katie Pettibone, Stephanie Maxwell-Pierson,

Merritt Palm, Hannah Swett,

Stephanie Armitage-Johnson, Amy Baltzell,

Amy Fuller, Marci Porter, Sarah Bergeron, Lisa

Charles, Joan Touchette, Merritt Carey,

Sarah Cavanagh, Linda Lindquist,

Susanne Leech-Nairn, J. J. Isler.

After successfully defending the America's Cup in 1992 with the technology-driven *America³* juggernaut, Bill Koch sought a new challenge.

"I didn't want to do the same thing," said Koch. "I asked myself, 'What can I do differently?' Then it came to me." Make history—form the first all-women's America's Cup crew. The program was announced March 4, 1994. Within days, more than 600 women filed applications with *America³*, which invited 120 candidates to a series of trial sessions in San Diego.

The women came from a wide variety of backgrounds. Many had small-boat sailing experience and some were national and Olympic champions. But many of the members of the final 32-women team came from diverse sports like rowing and weight-lifting.

The only member of the crew with previous America's Cup experience was Dawn Riley, who sailed with the *America³* crew in trial races leading up to the 1992 America's Cup. Riley and helmswoman/skipper Leslie Egnot became the leaders of the women's team.

Said Egnot: "We don't want to be remembered as the first women's team. We want to be remembered as the defender."

Using the *Kanza* and *America³* hulls carried over from the '92 campaign, the women's team drilled almost daily beginning in June.

Their first official outing was a success. During the 1994 IACC World Championship, the women beat everyone around the course in the last San Diego Bay race and finished second to *oneAustralia* in the official offshore series.

Early in the defense trials, the women were handicapped not by their gender but by their boat. While both rivals had new boats, the women sailed the first three round-robins with 1992 champion *America³*. The women's on-the-water performance improved dramatically with the arrival of the new *Mighty Mary* before the fourth round-robin.

However, the start of the last round-robin also brought controversy when Dave Dellenbaugh came aboard as the only man on the crew. Dellenbaugh, who was starting helmsman and tactician on *America³* in 1992, replaced tactician J. J. Isler.

While it was no longer the all-women's team, "the women plus Dave" continued to impress rivals . . . right up to the last leg of the last race of the Citizen Cup.

Ahead of Dennis Conner's *Stars & Stripes* by 4:08 at the last mark, *Mighty Mary* lost by 52 seconds. A victory would have put *Mighty Mary* in a sail-off with *Young America* to determine which defended the America's Cup. The comeback sent Conner's team to the America's Cup.

San Diego's Playground

From the Point to the Peaks

An Italian journalist visiting the America's Cup was trying to get a "feel" for San Diego.

"What kind of a place is this?" wondered Luca Bontempelli.

"There are people playing in the snow and other people swimming at the beach on the same day. At the same time . . . people are running marathons, playing baseball, and racing motorcycles." That's San Diego . . . so many things going on at one time.

Yes, San Diego fronts on the Pacific Ocean and much of its heritage, commerce, and recreation is linked to the sea. But San Diego also faces Mexico, the mountains, the desert, and Los Angeles.

A one-word description of the United States's sixth-largest city would be "diverse" in everything.

"San Diego offers a wider variety of outdoor activities than any other city I've ever visited," native San Diegan Dennis Conner said in 1991.

At the time, Conner was discussing the America's Cup and San Diego and how to make the event work in his hometown. Conner knew it wouldn't be easy.

In 1990, the city of San Diego had a population of 1.1 million. The County of San Diego had a population of 2.5 million. The area is vast—4,255 square miles stretching east/west from the desert to the sea and north/south from sprawling Orange County to the Mexican border.

Over the last three decades, San Diego has almost doubled in size. And because the region is blessed with one of the world's best climates—an average temperature of 63 degrees with just under 10 inches of rain in most years—more than 33 million tourists visit the area annually.

The city's front porch is the Pacific Ocean with its miles of beaches. But the region also has 120 parks and 70 golf courses, plus countless tennis courts and swimming pools.

Clearly, San Diegans look outdoors for their recreation. Nielsen surveys routinely show that television viewing in San Diego is below that of the rest of America.

So, where is the best place to get a "feel" for San Diego?

Possibly the Cabrillo National Monument on Point Loma. After all, just below this point is where Juan Rodriguez Cabrillo, a Portuguese explorer sailing from Spain, landed in 1542. Cabrillo didn't "discover" San Diego, though. Indians had lived in the area for centuries, mostly along the banks of the river that runs through Mission Valley.

But 50 years after the first voyage of Columbus, San Diego is where California began.

The Cabrillo National Monument offers visitors a panoramic view of most of what San Diego has to offer.

Facing west, you feel the sea breeze that air-conditions the city. And just off the beaches of Point Loma are the courses that hosted all three of San Diego's America's Cup defenses.

Turning south, you look down upon the entrance to San Diego Bay—one of the world's great natural harbors. Cabrillo anchored off what is now Ballast Point on the southeast side of Point Loma near this entrance to the harbor.

Look beyond the water to Coronado and you find the North Island Naval Air Station and a row of aircraft carriers on the east side of Coronado. San Diego remains one of the world's largest naval facilities. Farther south on Coronado is the majestic Hotel del Coronado, one of the world's largest wood structures. Built in 1888, it is a designated National Historic Landmark and during the 1995 races it played host to the America's Cup Ball.

To the east of the Hotel del Coronado is the 2.2-mile Coronado bridge. Built in 1969, it links San Diego to Coronado—and the city's past to its future. On the other end of the Coronado Bay Bridge is downtown San Diego, the revived heart of the area.

Tucked between new skyscrapers and adjacent to San Diego's harborfront Convention Center is the Gaslamp District, an eclectic and electric mix of pubs, bistros, and restaurants that dances nightly to myriad beats.

Look beyond the skyline to the east and you discover the mountains of the Laguna and Cuyamaca ranges. With peaks more than a mile high, the mountains are tipped with

*O*n May 4, 1995, the historic Hotel del Coronado (opposite) served as the site of the America's Cup Ball. On May 5, the stage at Embarcadero Marina Park South (below) provided the perfect backdrop for the America's Cup Opening Ceremonies. The Pointer Sisters and a fly-by of F-18 Hornets from Miramar Naval Air Station followed the introduction of the teams. Although the skies didn't cooperate completely, the light rain left the area in time for the next day's opening race.

snow in the winter and feature some of the nation's top year-round hiking trails. Beyond the mountains is the Anza-Borrego desert, home each spring to a wildflower bloom that attracts visitors from around the world. The desert is truly one of San Diego's sandboxes, a playground for children of all ages who cover the terrain by foot or on a variety of vehicles.

On certain magical days each winter, it is possible to enjoy a desert sunrise, frolic in the mountain snow, and take a dip in the Pacific Ocean.

As your eyes fall back toward the San Diego skyline, the greenbelts dominate the panorama. The most notable is just north of downtown—Balboa Park, a 1,400-acre retreat of museums and gardens in the heart of the city. Here, museums are housed in baroque-style buildings originally built for the 1915-16 Panama-California Exposition and the 1935-36 California-Pacific International Exposition.

*O*f all the innovations for the 1995 America's Cup, the Port of San Diego's America's Cup Pavilion adjacent to America's Cup Harbor on Shelter Island proved to be one of the more popular. More than 110,000 people visited the pavilion, which opened just before the start of the Louis Vuitton Cup and Citizen Cup finals and remained open through the end of the America's Cup.

A focal point of Balboa Park is the world-famous San Diego Zoo—home to one of the world's largest collections of mammals, birds, and reptiles, in addition to housing a large display of tropical flowers and trees. Wildlife is a recurring theme in San Diego. And 30 miles to the north of the city is the San Diego Zoo's Wild Animal Park—where the animals roam free and the humans are transported through various regions by monorail. Marine lovers can visit the new Steven Birch Aquarium in La Jolla or Sea World on Mission Bay.

The Mission Bay Aquatic Park is the largest single recreation area in San Diego, covering 4,600 acres with areas dedicated to sailing, water skiing, swimming, fishing, and camping. The Quivira Basin area near the ocean entrance to Mission Bay was home to six America's Cup syndicates in 1995 and four in 1992.

Now let your eyes drift back across Mission Valley to San Diego Jack Murphy Stadium—home of the baseball Padres and football Chargers, whose first trip to the Super Bowl paralleled the early stages of the 1995 America's Cup trials. Spectator sports play a major role in San Diego, which is also home to two major golf tournaments, college football's Holiday Bowl, thoroughbred horse racing at the Del Mar track and the annual unlimited hydroplane race on Mission Bay.

But the accent is on participation.

San Diegans enjoy their unique corner of the world and make the most of it. During the America's Cup, Shelter Island—one of two man-made, recreation-oriented

islands on North San Diego Bay—became a mecca.

Shelter Island also is home to one of the nation's largest sportsfishing fleets and to the San Diego Yacht Club.

Long before winning the America's Cup, the San Diego Yacht Club already was recognized as one of the world's premier yacht clubs. The club itself is part of San Diego's history.

As a city, San Diego dates back to 1769 when Don Gaspar de Portola led a group of soldiers into the area to establish a fort and a mission led by Father Junipero Serra. A century later, Alonzo Horton oversaw the move of San Diego's heart from what is now known as Old Town to its present site. The arrival of the Santa Fe Railroad in 1885 caused San Diego's population to quadruple in a year. A year later, both the San Diego Rowing Club and San Diego Yacht Club were founded.

In its formative years, the San Diego Yacht Club struggled. It split into two clubs, had problems finding a permanent home and was in debt. The club moved nine times before arriving at its present Point Loma site in 1923.

The modern history of the San Diego Yacht Club parallels the life of Joe Jessop. In 1928, Jessop established the junior sailing program that became the training ground for a cadre of world champions. That same year he also introduced the Star class sloop to San Diego, which, over the years, has become synonymous with the San Diego Yacht Club.

Jessop also helped lead the West Coast into the America's Cup arena in 1967. Before the San Diego Yacht Club won the America's Cup, it had actively participated in six campaigns.

The first West Coast defense effort was launched here in 1967 with the modified 12-Meter *Columbia*. In 1974, Gerry Driscoll remodified two-time champion *Intrepid* in his Shelter Island yard, trained all winter off Point Loma and nearly earned the right to defend over the new aluminum *Courageous*. San Diego then supplied the skipper and became the winter home to three straight New York Yacht Club America's Cup defense efforts—1977: *Enterprise* (Lowell North and Gerry Driscoll), 1980: *Freedom* (Dennis Conner), and 1983: *Liberty* (Conner).

Then Conner launched his own challenge out of the San Diego Yacht Club for 1987. *Stars & Stripes* won in Australia and brought the America's Cup to San Diego.

The homegrown roster of the San Diego Yacht Club reads like a Who's Who of sailing . . . Conner, North, Burnham, Driscoll, Mark Reynolds, Carl Eichenlaub, Brian Ledbetter, J. J. Isler and others . . . many, many others.

In 1910, San Diego Yacht Club purchased the Silver Gate from civic leader John B. Spreckels. The former ferryboat served as the club-house at the foot of Hawthorn Street and later on Coronado before it developed dry rot and had was scrapped. San Diego Yacht Club moved nine times before arriving at its present site in 1923.

FOLLOWING PAGES:

On a beautiful day in San Diego, the mountains are visible in the distance from Point Loma. In the foreground, the San Diego Yacht Club is nestled on the shores of the bay.

A CUP LIKE NO OTHER

MEMORABLE MOMENTS AND MISHAPS

America's Cup '95 will always be remembered for the phenomenal run of New Zealand's *Black Magic*.

The numbers speak volumes:

A 5-0 sweep of Team Dennis Conner on the borrowed *Young America* in an America's Cup series that saw the Russell Coutts-skippered *Black Magic* lead at every mark.

And a 37-1 on-the-water record in the Louis Vuitton Cup challenger trials . . . the only loss being by 15 seconds.

However, Team New Zealand's remarkable march to victory was but one chapter of a saga that set America's Cup '95 apart from the previous 28 defenses.

A new twist in the story line appeared almost daily.

The first women's team. The first sinking. The first intrusion by an aircraft carrier.

France 2 was dropped on the ground . . . then later lost its keel and fell over. *France 3* was dismasted. First a tornado, then a rogue wave crippled *Young America*. *Stars & Stripes* limped home after almost losing its keel and sinking. Next came the compromise sending all three defenders to the finals of the Citizen Cup.

Then there was the weather. Three years ago, not a single day of racing was lost to the weather. In 1995, 19 days were disrupted or lost. Both the America's Cup fleet and the city of San Diego struggled through an unseasonably cold and wet winter that sent meteorologists scurrying to their record books. There were days of too much wind and perilously high seas . . . followed immediately by becalmed days.

The America's Cup ended with *Black Magic* sailing away from the competition, but much will be also be remembered from the on-shore activities that were organized as a part of the 1995 event.

"It was truly a new atmosphere for the America's Cup in San Diego," commented Chuck Nichols, president of America's Cup '95. "This was the user-friendly America's Cup and I think we honestly learned how to do it right."

From the first few days that planning for the event began, in late 1992, America's Cup '95 organizers worked successfully to develop and implement a central focus for activities on Shelter Island. "The support and response we received from the community were tremendous," said Nichols, "and with the help of our sponsors we were able to create an exciting center of gravity on Shelter Island which thousands of visitors were able to enjoy."

During the 1995 event, Shelter Island played host to the Port of San Diego America's Cup Pavilion, the America's Cup '95 Concert Series at Humphrey's, the America's Cup Club at the Bali Hai, the Louis Vuitton America's Cup Media Centre and the America's Cup '95 Headquarters. All were within walking distance of each other, providing the public with a greatly enhanced ability to get involved with the event.

But the excitement for the event began with the women—and a press conference in New York City in March of 1994. Sixty weeks before the culminating race, Bill Koch made history with a team that drew even more attention than the Kiwis—the first women's crew ever to race for the America's Cup.

The America³ team won deserved accolades. But there was controversy, too. On the morning of the first semifinals race, Bill Koch broke up the all-women's crew—putting 1992 tactician Dave Dellenbaugh aboard the new *Mighty Mary*, replacing J. J. Isler. The first "all-women's" crew became the "women's team." Still quite an accomplishment . . . if not quite the same. Throughout the trials, the women—some of whom had never sailed before they joined the program—sailed beyond expectations. Eight months of nonstop training had transformed the crew into a highly competitive team. The women were in the running for the right to defend right up until the last day—make that the last leg—of the Citizen Cup.

In another incredible twist to America's Cup '95, Dennis Conner's *Stars & Stripes* rallied from a 4:08 deficit on the last leg to defeat *Mighty Mary* by 52 seconds. It was the greatest last-leg comeback in America's Cup history. It also clinched for Conner the right to defend the America's Cup.

"I'm exceptionally proud of the women," said Koch. "They performed exceptionally well. They were tough enough and smart enough." Said Egnot: "I thought we did a great job."

But perhaps the best evaluation of the first women's campaign came from backup navigator Annie Nelson, who, in the wake of elimination said: "We didn't lose because we

The America's Cup International Broadcast Center (below) provided television signals off the water for both live and delayed broadcasts around the world. In the United States, returning once again to provide its award-winning coverage, ESPN brought a number of innovations to the 1995 event including their greatly enhanced SailTrack graphics, on-board microphones and yacht cams. In New Zealand, TV New Zealand garnered one of the largest ever television audiences in the country's history.

*S*an Diego's weather experts said the January 4, 1995, storm wasn't a tornado. But one Young America *spinnaker landed in the Sea World parking lot a mile to the east, while a genoa was flung north into Mission Bay's Quivira Basin. Worse, the destroyed sail loft (foreground) was thrown against the hull of* Young America, *causing $600,000 damage to the mermaid. Said skipper Kevin Mahaney: "Rather than kill our campaign the storm made us stronger. We went from being individuals to being a team."*

*T*he French were lifting France 2 into Mission Bay for the first time on the morning of December 7, 1994, when the interior lift box failed and France 2 *(to the right of '92 challenger* Ville de Paris*) crashed to the ground. When asked by a reporter if the damage was significant, French coach Harold Cudmore replied: "These things aren't basketballs."*

*A*lthough relegated to a role of trial horse, France 2 was on an important mission testing a radical new mainsail February 20, 1995, when the keel fell off the boat. As France 2 fell slowly over on its side, helmsman Thierry Peponnet scrambled to the high side, pulled out his cellular phone and called skipper Marc Pajot back at the French basecamp. "I have bad news, Marc. Come get us. The keel has fallen off and we could be sinking."

As water poured into the cockpit, helmsman Rod Davis asked co-designer and mainsheet trimmer Iain Murray: "Big fella, are we sinking? . . . My God, we're sinking." The March 5, 1995, sinking of oneAustralia *was the most memorable scene from America's Cup '95. In the top frame, a catastrophic crack appears across the width of* oneAustralia's *hull just aft of the mast. As crewmen jump for safety, the boat folds in two and slides under the surface in two horrific minutes.*

are women . . . we lost because that was the way it was."

And the way it was for most of America's Cup '95 was unusual. A chronological sampling of some of the more unusual incidents of the 29th defense:

December 7, 1994—As the recently arrived *France 2* was being crane-lifted into the water for the first time, the boat plunged 15 feet onto the tarmac of the team's Mission Bay compound. The force of the impact drove the keel blade up through the hull and deck. It took the French almost a month and $1 million to rebuild the boat.

January 4, 1995—At 9:30 p.m., powerful tornado-like winds from a Pacific storm skipped over the five other compounds on Mission Bay, but cut a swath through PACT 95—toppling trees and destroying the team's sail loft and hospitality structures. The sail loft was thrown into *Young America,* which was sitting in its cradle alongside the loft. The boat was lifted out of its cradle, twisted, and dropped back into the cradle at an angle causing a dozen puncture wounds and internal damage. It took the team 10 days to repair the damage.

January 17—NZL-39 crewman Steve Cotton loses the tips of two fingers on his left hand after the hand is caught in a block during a close race between rival New Zealand challengers. The tips are retrieved, but cannot be reattached. Cotton is racing again before the trials end—becoming the first injured Kiwi crewman to show amazing recuperative powers. Team New Zealand crewmen Warwick Fleury (appendectomy) and Jeremy Scantlebury (hernia) both are sailing within weeks of major surgery.

February 4—As the first pair of challengers are starting in a heavy fog, the 1,092-foot, 94,000-ton U.S. aircraft carrier *Abraham Lincoln* appears like a ghost ship out of the gloom and parks in the middle of the starting area. Despite the latest in navigational aides, the carrier picks up no warning messages from the Coast Guard. The scene is surrealistic . . . the challenger fleet warily keeping its distance as the carrier glides away back into the fog. Said *oneAustralia* helmsman Rod Davis upon seeing the carrier lurch out of the mist: "My God, Dennis [Conner] does have a new boat."

February 20—French Follies II. After a day of racing, *France 2,* now the team's trial horse, is testing against *France 3* seven miles west of Mission Bay. As dusk approaches, helmsman Thierry Peponnet feels the wheel on *France 2* get lighter as the 75-foot sloop slowly begins to roll over on its side. The 20-ton keel has fallen off. No one is injured and rapid action by the French crew and rival teams save *France 2* from sinking.

March 5—OneAustralia sinks. While racing *Black Magic* in storm-whipped seas, *oneAustralia's* hull suddenly cracks on both sides just behind the mast. The boat quickly folds in two and the $3 million hull rapidly sinks, disappearing under the surface in two minutes. It is a bad day all around. *France 3* is dismasted. *Mighty Mary* breaks a forward brace in the bow. But *oneAustralia* is the first boat in America's Cup history to sink. As water pours in, the crew jumps for safety and is quickly retrieved by Australian and New Zealand chase boats. Miraculously, no one is injured. But the scene is haunting.

March 12—While being towed out of Mission Bay for a practice, *Young America* hits a rogue, 12-foot wave and suffers extensive damage to the underside of the hull. A 16-foot by 4-foot section between the bow and front edge of the keel delaminates. The boat limps back to its compound for six more days of repairs.

March 18—The America's Cup again makes national headlines as Koch replaces J. J. Isler with a man in an effort to add a crewman with America's Cup experience in the afterguard. *Mighty Mary* is no longer an all-women's crew and the presence of Dave Dellenbaugh stirs reaction far beyond the America's Cup family.

March 26—The keel almost falls off *Stars & Stripes* midway through a race. As the crew stuff sail bags into the hole between the keel and the bottom of the hull, pumps are put aboard the boat and flotation and marker buoys are raised to the top of the mast. The crew breaks out the life jackets as the boat is towed slowly back to its base.

*P*umps pull water out of the bowels of Stars & Stripes *after the keel almost fell off the the boat during a March 26 race. Said helmsman Paul Cayard: "I'm not joking when I say the boat could have sunk . . . we were lucky to get it back to the dock."*

FOLLOWING PAGES:

The crew of Nippon *look up toward the bow of the* Abraham Lincoln *after the 1,092-foot aircraft carrier emerged out of a fog bank on February 4, 1995, and parked in the middle of the challenger's starting line.*

April 4—Hours before *Stars & Stripes* and *Mighty Mary* are to meet in a sail-off to determine which will face *Young America* in the defense finals, a deal is brokered to keep all three alive. Instead of being eliminated in the sail-off, *Stars & Stripes* survives through the compromise and goes on to win the right to defend. PACT 95 has opened the door to its own demise. Said PACT 95 president John Marshall: "We ran the possibilities through a computer and this deal is good for us."

April 26—Perhaps the greatest comeback in America's Cup history. Conner's team needs a win over *Mighty Mary* in the last scheduled race of the Citizen Cup finals to earn the right to defend. A *Stars & Stripes* loss would send *Mighty Mary* into a one-race sail-off with *Young America. Stars & Stripes* trails by 4:08 starting the run to the finish. *Stars & Stripes* wins by 52 seconds. Of the comeback, Conner says one word: "Amazing."

April 30—Conner makes the difficult decision to park *Stars & Stripes* and defend the America's Cup with *Young America.* The boat switch is unprecedented. Conner's crew has less than a week to train aboard *Young America.*

May 13—Team New Zealand completes its 5-0 sweep of Team Stars & Stripes aboard *Young America.*

THE IACC WORLD CHAMPIONSHIP

AN UPBEAT PREVIEW TO THE CUP

The second International America's Cup Class World Championship was supposed to be a dress rehearsal for America's Cup '95.

The October 28-November 5, 1994 event was that—and much more. The 1994 IACC Canterbury of New Zealand World Championship set the stage for the most successful of San Diego's three America's Cup events.

"I'd like to think the Worlds raised the awareness of the America's Cup in San Diego," said Bob Spriggs, the chairman of the regatta. "I believe the general San Diego public enjoyed the 1995 [America's Cup] event much more than they did San Diego Yacht Club's first two defenses and I think the . . . Worlds played a role in that success."

They did—particularly the three exhibition races sailed on San Diego Bay on two consecutive weekends.

"The Worlds . . . set an upbeat tone for the America's Cup," said Dennis Conner. "People who had no idea about the size of the boats or the scope of the event got a close view."

Although the officially scored World Championship—which was dominated by *oneAustralia*—was sailed in the ocean off San Diego, three exhibition races, the San Diego Bay Series, were sailed in the San Diego Bay right off the streets of downtown San Diego.

Here, with races for the America's Cup having for years been sailed off somewhere . . . off Newport, Rhode

Island; off Fremantle, Western Australia; and off San Diego, America's Cup '95 organizers wanted to bring the feel of America's Cup racing closer to the city of San Diego.

The San Diego Bay Series didn't just happen, though. The idea had to be individually sold to each of the seven competing teams. "Originally, I had some trepidation about racing these boats on San Diego Bay," said Conner. "But it was really good for the event."

However, even on the morning of the first two San Diego Bay races, America's Cup '95 officials were concerned about the reception. Would people turn out for what was, in reality, an exhibition?

They did. On a sunny Sunday afternoon, October 30, approximately 15,000 San Diegans got the closest view possible of America's Cup Class boats. The downtown Broadway Pier—site of Bank of America's "Party on the Pier" —was packed and spectators also lined nearby Harbor and Shelter islands to watch the 75-foot sloops race in close quarters.

Many got more than they expected. Conner's *Stars & Stripes* sailed into the fingers between the downtown shipping piers. Kevin Mahaney followed with *Spirit of Unum*. Soon, *oneAustralia*, *Nippon*, and the women's team on *America³* were literally sailing under the eyes of somewhat astonished spectators.

Dennis Conner put on a show for San Diegans who turned out October 30 for the "Party on the Pier" gala surrounding the first two races of the San Diego Bay Series. Conner drove his USA-11 between the B Street and Broadway piers, giving spectators a real closeup of the International America's Cup Class boats.

Then again, for the third and final San Diego Bay race six days later, a slightly larger crowd turned out to watch the women of *America³* win their first race.

Said *oneAustralia* skipper John Bertrand: "I thought the bay races gave the general public an excellent opportunity to connect with our event. Certainly, that was good. And we should endeavor to do something like this again."

Clearly, the 1994 IACC World Championship brought the America's Cup into sharper focus within the San Diego community. It also served as a coming out party for the first all-women's crew in America's Cup history and introduced the Russians to IACC racing.

Before the World Championship, the women's team hadn't raced an IACC sloop in competition. *America³* finished second to *oneAustralia* in the official ocean series and was first across the finish line in the third San Diego Bay race—although all three American entrants were disqualified for sailing outside the perimeter of the course while giving the interested public a better view.

"The Worlds proved to everyone, including ourselves, that we could handle our boat in the closest of quarters and be competitive with the world's best," said Leslie Egnot, who co-skippered *America³* in the World Championship.

As for the Russians, they came, they saw, and they sailed . . . not very fast, but they

*D*ominating was the only word to describe oneAustralia's *performance in the* World Championship. *John Bertrand's challenge entered its first new hull—the long and narrow AUS-31—in the series. Helmed by Rod Davis,* oneAustralia *easily won the official World Championship, which was sailed off Point Loma.*

*C*learly, the closest and most exciting races of the Worlds were the three sailed on San Diego Bay. Here, the women of America³ lead the fleet downwind toward the Coronado Bay Bridge. Following are Dennis Conner's Stars & Stripes, *the two Japanese entries, one*Australia, *and the Russians.*

sailed. Unaccepted as a late challenger in 1992 and unable to fund a 1995 America's Cup campaign, the Russians leased the first IACC boat built by the Italians to sail in the World Championship. After less than a full day of practice, the crew led by Sergei Borodinov went racing. On the first two days, the Russians failed to finish in the allowed time. Then they finished last in every race.

"But we did what we set out to do," said Borodinov. "We raced on San Diego Bay where no Russian had sailed before. And we raced on an America's Cup boat, where no Russian had sailed before."

Only two boats built for the 1995 America's Cup raced in the World Championship. Bertrand's *oneAustralia* (AUS-31), helmed by Rod Davis, won the Worlds with four straight—and decisive—victories in the ocean. The other new boat wasn't so fortunate. Nippon's JPN-30 was dismasted a week before the World Championship began and missed the first weekend of racing. Still, *Nippon '94*, skippered by Peter Gilmour, finished third in the final standings behind the women of America[3].

Like the America's Cup trials to follow, the World Championship was sailed in a variety of conditions—and two races were cancelled due to weather.

The conditions didn't matter to *oneAustralia,* however. Bertrand's crew led at 20 of the 24 marks in the ocean races and posted the fleet's fastest time on half the legs.

"We're bloody happy," Bertrand said after *oneAustralia* completed the sweep. "The Worlds are only a small step. But we came out to see where we are . . . and it's good to see that we're not behind. It was an important exercise for our crew. Those who haven't been here before now have a taste of the variety of conditions San Diego offers."

One of the newcomers to San Diego was *oneAustralia* tactician Glenn Bourke, who struck a theme that would be repeated throughout the America's Cup.

"We saw a full range of conditions," said Bourke. "Our meteorologist gave us five variations every day and really wasn't sold on any of them. Even if you guess right, there are 30-degree shifts and big holes . . . and the seas. It is easy to see why so many world champions came out of San Diego. Anything else is a step down in education."

The San Diego Bay Series was won by the John Cutler-skippered *Nippon '92* (JPN-26). *OneAustralia* finished second and *America*[3] was third. "Considering everything we've been through, the dismasting and repairs, we are very, very happy," said Cutler.

*S*kipper John Bertrand (foreground) holds the IACC World Championship trophy above his head after oneAustralia celebrated its long-awaited arrival in San Diego with a victory.

FOLLOWING PAGES:

San Diego's downtown skyline proved a perfect backdrop for the three-race San Diego Bay Series. Nippon *sails downwind past the Convention Center en route to the San Diego Bay Series championship. Trailing are PACT 95's* Spirit of Unum, oneAustralia, *the second Japanese entry, and the Russians .*

BELOW:

Nippon *skipper John Cutler accepts the $25,000 check going to the winner of the San Diego Bay Series. The prize was divided among the Japanese crew members.*

THE LOUIS VUITTON CUP

CHALLENGER RACES FOR THE AMERICA'S CUP

Politely, they turned down an invitation to sail in the 1994 World Championship.

And when they arrived in San Diego, they did so with little fanfare. Quickly and quietly, the members of Team New Zealand set up their base on America's Cup Harbor and went to work.

That in itself was not unusual. All seven challengers were busy the month before the start of the Louis Vuitton Cup.

Pedro Campos and Chris Dickson were struggling just to get their respective Spanish and New Zealand efforts to San Diego.

The French and Japanese challenges were rebuilding the first new boats each constructed for the 1995 campaign. Toiling behind closed doors, an army of Japanese workers made "extensive modifications" to the JPN-30 hull, which had been dismasted before the Worlds. The French were repairing the crippled *France 2*, which had been dropped December 7 while being lifted into Mission Bay for the first time.

The spotlight was on the cooperating Australian syndicates. *OneAustralia* had survived a challenge that its partnership with Syd Fischer's Australian Challenge had violated the rule limiting each team to two new boats for America's Cup '95. *OneAustralia* had won the World Championship. Now the Australians practiced together daily as John Bertrand's powerful team awaited the arrival of its final boat.

Meantime, Team New Zealand went about its business. The crew would arrive at its compound early each morning, quickly put its two black-hulled sloops in the water and go sailing. Routinely, the boats, officially numbered NZL-32 and NZL-38, but both called *Black Magic,* would stay out past dark. Their nightly return to base, two black hulls towed silently in behind the tender, was eerie . . . and foreboding.

Unlike past New Zealand campaigns, not much was said by Team New Zealand. "We are too busy getting ready to say much right now," syndicate director Peter Blake offered one morning. "We'll be in touch."

Perhaps, the less said the better.

New Zealand had made three previous America's Cup challenges. All were launched with much ballyhoo. All got off to great starts. And all three failed.

"I think this effort will be different," trimmer Simon Daubney said one morning. "There's a different feel. The only thing that matters this time is the boat. Everything is centered on the boats."

The boats. The Kiwis spoke about them with a certain reverence. In time, the world would learn why. But the seeds of an exceptional campaign were planted long before the America's Cup or the Louis Vuitton Cup finals.

*C*hallenge of Record Committee chief executive officer Ernie Taylor (above left) and Louis Vuitton Malletier president Yves Carcelle preside over a scheduling draw prior to the challenger round-robins. Representing the boats (below, from left) are Marc Pajot (France), Dr. Peter Morris (oneAustralia), Syd Fischer (Sydney 95), Makoto Namba (Nippon), Chris Dickson (NZL-39), Russell Coutts (Black Magic), and Pedro Campos (Rioja de España) plus Louis Vuitton director of communications Jean-Marc Loubier.

"The secret is boring," Tom Schnackenberg said one day. Considered one of the brightest minds in the America's Cup game, Schnackenberg oversaw Team New Zealand's design program, which was co-chaired by naval architects Laurie Davidson and Doug Peterson.

"It's the teamwork. It sounds obvious. It is obvious. But it's not easy. Everything we put into the boat works together—the hull, the sails, the rig, the crew, the shore team, the appendages."

"When we started designing," said Peterson, "the crew asked Laurie and me for a boat that would be equal to what anyone else had. They didn't want tricks or anything fancy. They wanted to race. The crew wanted to win the America's Cup. The crew and designers worked together on the boat. We gave them an all-around boat. No breakthrough. Just solid all around. I think we won the America's Cup before the trials began."

Said mainsheet trimmer Warwick Fleury: "From day one, we liked our boat."

During those long practice sessions off San Diego, the *Black Magic* crew saw what it had . . . and knew it was good.

*O*n the first day of the Louis Vuitton Cup trials, Nippon's *remodeled JPN-30 hull scored an upset with a 66-second victory over IACC World Champion* oneAustralia. *Although the boats were side by side while nearing the first leeward mark,* Nippon *(top) had the inside right-of-way at the rounding.*

*C*hris Dickson drove both the boat and his small-budget challenge. Designed by Bruce Farr, the sharply bowed NZL-39 narrowly missed making the Louis Vuitton Cup finals an all- New Zealand affair. Dickson's team was the only semifinalist lacking a training partner, which, with the team's limited resources, proved to be a fatal handicap.

ROUND ONE

The challengers entered the first of four round-robins facing a new question.

For the first time in the quarter-century of multinational challenges, the challengers didn't have to pick their ultimate weapons before the start of the trials. Each had until April 9—the agreed upon common declaration date—to name their final boat.

For Spain, Dickson and Sydney 95, the question was moot. Theirs were one-boat campaigns. And the new *oneAustralia* and *Nippon* hadn't yet reached San Diego.

So only Team New Zealand had to make a decision. On the eve of the commencement of racing, Blake named the newer NZL-38 to represent New Zealand.

The selection raised questions. There had been rumors from New Zealand that the nation's unsuccessful 1992 challenger (NZL-20) had been faster than NZL-32 in a series of tests. The newer NZL-38 hadn't been sailed until the team reached San Diego. Speculation was rampant. Was Team New Zealand off pace? Said Bruce Farr, the designer for Michael Fay's first three challengers, including NZL-20: "We'll never see NZL-32 on the race course and they know the reason why." It should be noted that Farr was Dickson's designer in 1995. It should also be noted that, ultimately, he was wrong.

As in 1992, the first day of the Louis Vuitton Cup produced a pair of surprises. The "new" *Nippon* upset *oneAustralia,* and *Sydney 95* came from behind on the last leg to defeat *France 2.* A day later, *Sydney 95* beat Spain—giving Fischer more wins in 1995 than he had in all of the '92 trials.

The first of the "incidents" occurred the following day, on January 17. As Dickson's NZL-39 was gaining on its New Zealand rival on the run to the finish, crewman Steve Cotton caught his hand in a block and lost the tips of two fingers. Also on that day, *Nippon* beat *France 2.* It didn't seem to matter then, but later these teams would be vying to see which went to the semifinals and which went home sooner than expected.

Before the first round ended, both New Zealand challengers also would beat *oneAustralia.*

ROUND TWO

The first round-robin closed with more questions than answers.

Between rounds, *oneAustralia* reconfigured AUS-31 to put it back in its World Championship-winning trim. And the French announced they would switch sooner than planned to *France 3.* Although the repairs to *France 2* cost

A maverick among his America's Cup brethren, Syd Fischer, (below at left), returned for his fourth bid in 1995. In the first two days of racing, Fischer's Sydney 95 won twice as many races as his Challenge Australia won in 1992. Sydney 95 was fast when the wind climbed above 12 knots. Four different helmsmen drove Sydney 95 during the trials, including Colin Beashel (below at wheel).

FOLLOWING PAGES:

Close-quarter sailing was prevalent throughout the America's Cup trials. Helmsman Rod Davis steers oneAustralia past a television camera boat en route to the starting area during the Louis Vuitton Cup.

MEDIA

SWATH OCEAN

AWLGRIP

AMERICA'S CUP
CAMERA BOAT

France 2 *was a troublesome* *first time in San Diego. Then its keel fell off during a* *problem for Marc Pajot's French challenge through-* *sail test on February 20. The French campaign, which* *out the Louis Vuitton Cup. On December 7, the boat* *was partially funded by the French government,* *was dropped onto the tarmac of its Mission Bay* *failed to reach the semifinals causing controversy* *compound as it was being lifted into the water for the* *back home.*

almost $1 million and took a month to complete, the boat was not the boat it was before the December 7 crash.

Team New Zealand elected to stick with its undefeated NZL-38 for the second round. But the Kiwis would not remain quiet during the second round-robin. Team New Zealand found itself a party to three major protests during the round.

One would cost the Kiwis a victory.

During the first round of trials, the Kiwis adopted the practice of sending Murray Jones up the mast on light-wind days. Sitting on the top spreaders, Jones would help kick the mainsail battens over during tacks and jibes and look for those elusive patches of wind. Jones even took his lunch aloft and communicated with the crew through a radio line that ran down the mast.

But following a loss to *Black Magic* in the second race of the round, *oneAustralia* protested that Jones's position in the top spreader placed him outside the sheerline of the boat when *Black Magic* heeled. The jury ruled for *oneAustralia*. Henceforth, Jones spent much of his time aloft in the second spreaders.

There were two other sticky questions facing the international jury.

One raised the question about *Nippon* possibly violating the two-boat limit when it extensively modified JPN-30 following the Worlds. Would the soon-to-arrive JPN-41 really be a third new boat? The jury ruled in behalf of *Nippon*.

The other involved the 17th man position on the crew. Adopted in 1992 with the inception of the International America's Cup Class, the "17th man" was to be a "nonparticipating member of the crew." By design, that meant syndicate heads, sponsors, guests, and, on occasion, media.

But some teams began using the "17th man" as a platform for coaches and designers to study the boat and crew operations. This was particularly the case on *Nippon*. Former world match racing champion Peter Gilmour sailed aboard *Nippon* daily as coach after his bid to join the active crew was rejected by the international jury for failure to meet the two-year residency requirements. The class technical director eventually placed limitations on "technical personnel" sailing as the 17th man.

The second round will be remembered most for the surrealistic intrusion of the U.S. aircraft carrier *Abraham Lincoln* onto the course on February 4.

The first pair of challengers—*Black Magic* and *France 3*—had just started in limited visibility when the 1,092-foot, 94,000-ton Nimitz-class carrier ghosted out of the fog

Murray Jones stands on Black Magic's top spreader, scanning the horizon for those light and shifty San Diego breezes. Through the round-robins, Team New Zealand's only loss came when oneAustralia successfully protested the practice because Jones was outside the sheerline of Black Magic when the boat heeled. Thereafter, Jones usually searched for wind from the second spreader.

*T*he late-arriving Spanish were still learning the intricacies of their Rioja de España *when their run ended with the end of the* round-robins. *The Spanish closed a respectable 3-6 after losing their first 15 races.*

and parked almost in the middle of the Louis Vuitton Cup starting line.

Involved in operations to the southwest of San Diego, the *Abraham Lincoln* had been looking for an opening in the fog to launch several helicopters. Just before the first pair started, *oneAustralia* helmsman Rod Davis spotted the *Abraham Lincoln* approaching the race course.

"We kept calling the race committee and telling them they couldn't start," said Davis. "They told us, 'We're monitoring the situation.' I don't think they fully appreciated the situation."

Because IACC boats are carbon-fiber and the spectator and race committee fleets were at anchor or as motionless as possible, Navy officials said the carrier had problems picking up the America's Cup traffic on its radar. Captain Richard Nibe of the *Abraham Lincoln* said the first indication of trouble came when one of his spotters on the bow physically sighted a bright yellow Louis Vuitton Cup buoy marking one side of the course.

The second round of racing was marked by a strong comeback by *oneAustralia*, which lost only one race. *OneAustralia* and *Black Magic* both finished the round with 5-1 records. Although *oneAustralia* had defeated *Black Magic* via a protest, the only loss suffered by Bertrand's crew came via a breakdown against *Nippon*. Minutes after the start, an internal spreader bar broke inside the *oneAustralia* mast.

ROUND THREE

Bertrand was hoping to save the new AUS-35 for the fourth round-robin.

But the tight race for positioning behind *Black Magic* forced *oneAustralia* to show its trump card early.

Team New Zealand decided to stick with the NZL-38 hull. And *Nippon* elected to keep JPN-41 in reserve for one more round—a decision that almost proved costly.

By the time the penultimate round-robin ended, it was clear that Team New Zealand, Dickson's New Zealand challenge, and *oneAustralia* were headed to the semifinals.

The only question was who would fill out the field. And it was apparent the French were in big trouble.

The weather-interrupted round opened with *Sydney 95*—sailing in the 12-knot breezes it liked—leading wire-to-wire to upset *France 3* by 38 seconds. The loss stunned the French. "It was a race we could not afford to lose," said Pajot. "It was a very bad performance."

The loss dropped the French to sixth in the standings. It could have been worse. *Sydney 95* almost upset

What might have been—AUS-35 chases NZL-38 in the tight third-round match between the new oneAustralia *and Team New Zealand.* Black Magic *won by 26 seconds, although the margin between these two challengers was as little as eight seconds entering the final leg. The next time the boats met, AUS-35 sank.*

FOLLOWING PAGES:

The hard-working crew of NZL-39 came within two wins over oneAustralia *of making the Louis Vuitton Cup finals an all-New Zealand competition.*

Tws	Heel	Bsp
4	7	5.1
5	11	6.9
6	14	8.0
7	17	8.7
8	21	9.0
9	24	9.3
10	26	9.5
12	27	9.5
14	28	9.5
16	29	9.5

A Bayliner carrying a team of on-the-water umpires powers to a safe distance as Nippon (*above*) and NZL-39 engage in the ritualistic, prestart jockeying for position called "circling." The helmsmen involved—Nippon's *John Cutler and NZL-39's Chris Dickson—were childhood friends in Auckland and teammates with Nippon in 1992.*

As skipper Marc Pajot drives, the crew of France 3 trims the huge gennaker on the second boat the French built for the 1995 challenge. After making the semifinals in 1987 and 1992, the "bitterly disappointed" French were eliminated in the round-robins. "Simply, we were not good enough," said Pajot. "It's a failure we must accept and learn from."

Nippon, a result that would have dropped the French two wins out of fifth place.

After three straight losses to open the round, Pajot shook up his crew. He replaced himself on the helm with Francois Brenac, and Thierry Peponnet replaced reigning match racing world champion Bertrand Pacé as tactician.

On the first day of the switch, *France 3* lost a narrow decision to *oneAustralia*. But on the following day, NZL-39 beat the French by 6:23. The French were closer to last-place *Rioja de España* than to a semifinals berth.

Pajot put himself back on the wheel and brought Pacé back on the boat. The switch resulted in a victory over the Spanish on February 20.

Victory. And defeat.

Immediately following the finish of the February 20 race, *France 3* went sailing against *France 2*. It was supposed to be a routine sail test. It was anything but. Seventy-five minutes into the session, Peponnet felt the helm of *France 2* get light. Suddenly, the sloop began a slow roll over onto its side. Twenty tons of keel had fallen off the boat and plunged 900 feet to the ocean floor.

With the help of the Spanish, who lost the keel off their earliest design in 1991 and knew how to salvage a keelless IACC sloop, the French kept *France 2* afloat and slowly and safely towed the boat to its Mission Bay home.

But the blow crippled the French campaign. There wasn't another keel to be put on *France 2*. The boat would not be repaired. France would sail the rest of the trials without a tuning partner. "The loss of *France 2* as a trial horse might have been the fatal blow to our bid," said Pajot, whose team closed the round with two straight wins to climb back into fifth in the standings.

Chris Dickson (standing, yellow cap) drives NZL-39 into a moderate breeze as tactician Peter Lester (to Dickson's immediate right) scans the instruments. Although eliminated in the Louis Vuitton Cup semifinals, Dickson's boat had the second-best win-loss percentage in either fleet.

ROUND FOUR

The most poignant moment of the 1995 America's Cup was the sinking of *oneAustralia* on March 5.

Captured by ACTV, the scene was horrific—the 17 men on board jumping into the water as the new AUS-35 folded in two just aft of the mast and slid under the surface in two minutes.

Clearly, the Australians were in shock that night. But as Bertrand quickly added, "We come from a tough stock. Aussies don't collapse. This is a tough blow. But we'll go on from here and win the America's Cup."

Aussies have moxie. And a sense of humor. After watching the incredible film of *oneAustralia* sinking, syndicate chief executive officer Dr. Peter Morris said: "That answers the two-boat controversy. Now it's time to get to work."

Within hours, the *oneAustralia* crew was at work preparing AUS-31 to return to racing.

The America's Cup is an event filled with opposite forces. Rival teams rushed to help the Australians with parts and equipment . . . as they had helped the French and *Young America*. But when *oneAustralia* asked for an extra day off to prepare their boat for racing, the French objected.

You only help so far in the America's Cup . . . then it's every team for itself. *OneAustralia* was scheduled to meet the French on the following day, and the French desperately needed a victory to climb back into the race for the last semifinals berth. "I would like to say yes to the *oneAustralia* request, but I cannot," said Pajot. "I have my team to protect. I hope the Australians understand."

They did. For survival is part of the game.

OneAustralia did not make it out on the course the next day. It forfeited the match to the French. But it was back in two days. And three days after the sinking, *oneAustralia* scored one of the more important wins of the Louis Vuitton Cup—although it went little noticed because of events elsewhere on the course that afternoon of March 8.

To reach the semifinals, *France 3* needed a victory over *Sydney 95* combined with a *Nippon* loss to *Rioja de España*. The French won their race. And for two laps, *Rioja de España* led *Nippon*. The margin was as much as 51 seconds. At the second leeward mark, the Spaniards still were ahead by 24 seconds. The Japanese engaged the Spaniards in a furious tacking duel on the last weather leg. On the 14th tack, *Nippon* broke through to the favored left side of the course. On the 21st exchange, the Japanese forced *Rioja de España* to tack away in a leebow encounter. Six more tacks gave JPN-41 an 8-second lead at the mark. They gained another five seconds on the run.

By a margin of 13 seconds, *Nippon* made the semis and the French were done. "This is a failure for my team," said Pajot. "It is very hard for me. The boat was not fast enough."

Almost unnoticed that day was *oneAustralia's* 57-second victory over Dickson's NZL-39. Dickson was over the starting line early, giving Bertrand's boat a 44-second headstart. *OneAustralia* never relinquished the lead.

The outcome allowed *oneAustralia* to move into second ahead of NZL-39 in the final round-robin standings. Second place also gave *oneAustralia* a tiebreaker over NZL-39 should the two boats tie for second in the semifinals. At the time, it seemed like an afterthought of a wild day. It turned out to be important.

*M*akoto Namba (shown below) emerged as one of the more popular personalities of the Louis Vuitton Cup. Just before the trials began, Namba was named skipper of Nippon, *a move that was welcomed by the mixed Japanese/Anglo crew.* "Namba deserves to be named the skipper," *said helmsman John Cutler.* "Everyone on our boat respects Namba and what he brings to the program."

THE SEMIFINALS

Team New Zealand dropped its long-awaited bomb on the eve of the Louis Vuitton Cup semifinals.

The NZL-38 *Black Magic* was being parked. The older NZL-32—the boat Farr said we'd never see—would represent Team New Zealand in the semifinals against Nippon's JPN-41, *oneAustralia's* surviving AUS-31, and Dickson's NZL-39.

"When I read Farr's comments months ago, I was very upset," said Davidson. "I knew NZL-32 was a good boat. During those trials in New Zealand, when it looked like NZL-20 was faster, well, what can I say . . . we were letting NZL-20 win to throw people off."

Still, some saw the switch as a gamble. NZL-38 had been unbeaten on the water throughout the round-robins. Said Blake: "We are comfortable with our decision."

It quickly became evident why.

The semifinals were a quadruple round-robin. The NZL-32 *Black Magic* never lost a race. Nine starts, nine wins. When it retired early from the semifinals to get back to the intrateam, two-boat testing that had propelled both *Black Magics* forward, NZL-32 had a four-win advantage over the closest opposition.

Only once did an opponent come closer than a minute to the Kiwis. Only once did a rival lead NZL-32 during the semifinals.

And that race offered a clue to the depth of *Black Magic* superiority.

On March 22, Davis won the start against Team New Zealand skipper Russell Coutts. Tacking expertly on the first weather leg, *oneAustralia* pulled out to a 64-second lead. NZL-32 battled back. At the end of the second run, *oneAustralia's* lead was down to 10 seconds.

Midway up the last weather leg, the boats were drag racing side by side with *oneAustralia* apparently safely to weather. But Coutts began climbing up on the leader. Soon, *Black Magic* was so close that *oneAustralia* was sailing in bad air and was forced to tack away. *Black Magic* won by 39 seconds. For the Kiwis, that was a close call.

Clearly, one boat deserved to be in the Louis Vuitton Cup finals. Sadly, another did not. Altered after barely making it into the semifinals, *Nippon* failed to win a race in the semifinals. At the end of the run, skipper Makoto Namba cried. "I apologize to all for not doing better," he said. "We tried very hard, but we could not win."

That left it up to two boats—*oneAustralia* and NZL-39. One would face

Team New Zealand's exemplary crew work throughout the Louis Vuitton Cup and the America's Cup offered few openings for the opposition. A spinnaker hoist (below) begins as Black Magic *rounds a weather mark during the 5-1 rout of* oneAustralia *in the finals. As* Black Magic *gains speed to weather (opposite), the crew crowds the high rail.*

FOLLOWING PAGES:

OneAustralia *and* Black Magic *beat into the wind during the final race of the Louis Vuitton Cup.*

Team New Zealand in the finals.

Dickson got the quick upper hand with a 79-second victory over *oneAustralia* in the first meeting of the pair. But *oneAustralia* won the next two meetings by 40 seconds and 1:43. The latter turned out to be decisive.

The pair were to meet each other on the final day of the semifinals. The race never happened. In the 11th of 12 rounds, *oneAustralia* defeated *Nippon* to move to 7-4. NZL-39 was 6-5. But had NZL-39 raced and beaten *oneAustralia* in the final race, the tiebreaker would have given the second berth in the finals to *oneAustralia*.

The semifinals reverted to the last race of the round-robins where *oneAustralia* clinched its place in the finals. "It is a sad way to be eliminated," said Dickson.

THE FINALS

During the break between the semifinals and finals, oneAustralia rebuilt AUS-31.

New bow. New transom. A slice was taken out of the aft section. And the boat was given a new bulb. It was a rush job. So much so that the lead keel bulb was shipped while still in a semimolten state . . . the heat setting fire to the truck transporting it from San Francisco. A 26-man crew—most of which was flown in from Australia—worked around the clock in three shifts remodeling AUS-31.

"We had to do something before the finals," said Davis. "It was evident we weren't going to win if things had remained as they were in the semifinals.

"The changes we made are a bid to get back into the game. Before AUS-35 sank, it was two minutes faster in two hours of sailing than this hull."

Ranking officers of the Miramar Naval Air Station joined America's Cup syndicate leaders, crewmen, race officials, and members of the international media when Fighter Town USA hosted the Louis Vuitton Party.

Bertrand knew the modifications were a gamble. They couldn't be tested. They should have made *oneAustralia* faster. But they also could have slowed the boat. The sword of design can cut both ways.

"Basically, we'll be sailing a new boat in the finals," said Davis. "I think we could lose a couple of races before we get it sorted out. The changes will make AUS-31 handle quite a bit different than it did before. But doing this is our best shot. Generally, it's not a good idea to make radical changes. But it's the only choice we have."

Three weeks later, Dennis Conner would be saying much the same thing.

OneAustralia was no match for Team New Zealand, which stuck with NZL-32 for the finals—meaning that it would also be the hull sailed in the America's Cup—provided the Kiwis won the Louis Vuitton Cup.

They did. By a 5-1 count.

John Bertrand's oneAustralia team won accolades for its tenacity. The syndicate quickly rebounded from the sinking of its new AUS-35. The older AUS-31 was racing within two days and scored an important victory over NZL-39 in its second race back. It then went on to earn the right to face Black Magic *in the Louis Vuitton Cup finals. "Our hats are off to oneAustralia," said Team New Zealand syndicate head Peter Blake. "I'm not sure we would have done as well with our boat going under."*

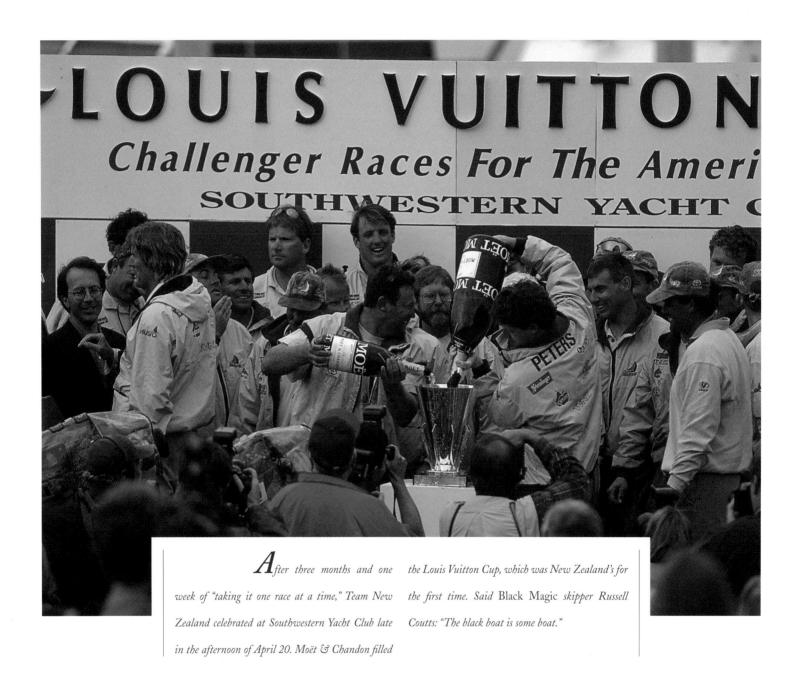

*A*fter three months and one week of "taking it one race at a time," Team New Zealand celebrated at Southwestern Yacht Club late in the afternoon of April 20. Moët & Chandon filled the Louis Vuitton Cup, which was New Zealand's for the first time. Said Black Magic *skipper* Russell Coutts: "The black boat is some boat."

Indeed, the Kiwis are mortal. In the fourth heat of the best 5-of-9, Davis kept *oneAustralia* ahead throughout perhaps the best race of the 1995 event.

OneAustralia never trailed . . . and never led by more than 18 seconds.

"Every time they made a run at us, we beat that puppy over the nose with a stick," said Davis. But the victory had ominous overtones for *oneAustralia* and the defenders.

OneAustralia won the start, had perfect tactics, called almost every shift right, had near flawless crew work—and won by 15 seconds.

"We'll bounce back," said *Black Magic* tactician Brad Butterworth. The Kiwis did. In two more races, the Louis Vuitton Cup was over. Team New Zealand, and its *Black Magic,* was headed to a date with destiny.

There was no New Zealand collapse in 1995.

"Sometimes," said Davis, "there is a danger to being real good, real early. You can peak too soon. I think New Zealand recognized this possibility from past campaigns.

"That is a really remarkable campaign. They win and they win. But I get a feeling they haven't peaked yet. Whenever they needed something extra, they had plenty in reserve."

In the 96 days between the start of the Louis Vuitton Cup and the fifth win over *oneAustralia,* Team New Zealand had sailed 234 legs. The Kiwis had led at the end of 215 of those legs and lost ground on only 56—half of those being when a victory had been safely tucked away.

Not once had *Black Magic* blown a lead.

Besides the race it won, *oneAustralia* had led at only one other mark during the finals—and Davis won all but one start.

"Russell doesn't worry about the starts," said Davis. "He just wants to keep his nose clean until the starting gun. Then he fires up the afterburners and takes off."

The margins in the Louis Vuitton Cup finals were almost what *Black Magic* willed them to be: 4:55, 1:57, 2:26, 3:54, and 2:13.

In defeat, Bertrand was philosophical:

"Team New Zealand put together an incredible campaign. Their attention to detail went from the top of the mast to the bottom of the keel.

"We will never know what would have happened if AUS-35 hadn't sunk. I think New Zealand will win the America's Cup. But I believe we would have beaten the defender, too."

Skipper Russell Coutts (left side of the Cup) and Team New Zealand syndicate director Peter Blake hold the Louis Vuitton Cup during ceremonies at the Louis Vuitton Media Centre. Flanking the Black Magic *leaders are, from left, Louis Vuitton America's Cup Media Centre operations director Bruno Troublé, Louis Vuitton Malletier director of communications Jean-Marc Loubier, and Louis Vuitton Malletier president Yves Carcelle.*

THE CITIZEN CUP

DEFENDER RACES FOR THE AMERICA'S CUP

Long before the first trials began in mid-January, interest in America's Cup '95 was at a record high.

The reason was obvious: The women.

"We're sailing in a fish bowl," sail trimmer Hannah Swett said one morning as the "Women's Team" prepared to go out for a routine practice session.

Routine?

Two national television crews and a bevy of photographers jockeyed for position on the docks to chronicle the women carrying bags of sails down to their two boats.

"It's pretty much like this every day," said Joan Touchette. "Every time we do something, you can hear the click of the cameras."

On May 16, 1992, Bill Koch's powerful, technology-driven *America³* captured the America's Cup. But it didn't capture the interest of the nation. Three years later, Koch had the entire world watching his team—long before it sailed a race.

The America's Cup was one of the last bastions of gender inequity. Over 28 defenses and 141 years, no woman had sailed in an actual America's Cup race in a working crew position.

Now there would be an entire boat of women vying for the right to defend the America's Cup. The Women's Team would take on Dennis Conner and the first-time PACT 95 defense candidates.

"I think it's great," Conner said of the women as the commencement of the defense trials approached.

"The women have certainly raised the awareness of the America's Cup. That is good for the event and the sport of sailing. How will they do? I think they'll be competitive."

That wasn't enough for the women. Certainly not for Leslie Egnot and Dawn Riley, who would emerge as the leaders of the *America³* crew.

The women of America³ (above) celebrate their historic defender trials-opening victory over Stars & Stripes with coach Kimo Worthington.

Early in the Citizen Cup, Dennis Conner (below in red sweater) could still be found at the wheel of Stars & Stripes.

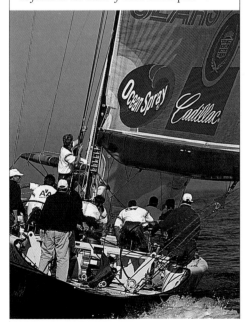

"I don't want people to look back on our campaign and say, 'The women did a nice job,'" said Egnot. "I want to win the trials and successfully defend the America's Cup. That is why I joined this program . . . not necessarily because we were going to be the first women to sail in the America's Cup."

"I think the mood of our boat parallels Leslie's thoughts," said Riley, who sailed with the *America³* crew during the 1992 trials but did not sail on the boat during the actual America's Cup—thus missing a date with history. "We don't want to be remembered just for being here . . . for being the first. We want to win."

But there they were, for the world to see . . . and that was history. Any doubts about the impact were dispelled on March 9, 1994 when Koch formally announced the Women's Team during a press conference in New York City.

No one knew what the future held for the experiment—certainly not some of the world champion women sailors originally named to the squad. Many were found wanting.

Sailing the huge International America's Cup Class sloops in quest of the America's Cup called for a different set of disciplines and skills than most women sailors had used in racing smaller classes—even in events such as the Olympics.

America³ had to find grinders and sewermen as well as helmsmen, trimmers, and navigators.

Koch opened his team to all applicants. More than 600 inquiries arrived. Kimo Worthington led a team of coaches held over from the 1992 championship team who culled the resumes and invited 120 women to San Diego for three tryout sessions. Only 30 women —enough to fill two crews—made the final cut.

A year before the 1995 America's Cup was scheduled to begin, an interesting cross-section of female athletes went to work in San Diego. There were rowers and weight-lifters as well as sailors. A few had never before been on a sailboat and many had never sailed in competition. Of those who had, few had big-boat experience.

"Early, just getting the boat around the course was a challenge," said bowman Susie Leech-Nairn. "Every day was a struggle. Everything was so much bigger than women sailors had ever worked with before. I think a lot of us were in awe of the boat at the beginning."

After months of training, Koch invited his 1992 crew to San Diego to engage the women in a series of trial races. The men won. Two months later, the '92 crew was invited back for a rematch. The women won. The women next made a strong showing in the World Championship—finishing second to *oneAustralia* in the official ocean series and leading the fleet around the course in the finale to the San Diego Bay series.

Still, the women were at a disadvantage as the trials approached. And it had nothing to do with gender. Both Team Dennis Conner and PACT 95 already had their new boats. The women's new boat wouldn't arrive until the start of the last round-robin.

But PACT 95 was lucky to have a boat. On the night of January 4—eight days before the scheduled first race of the defense trials—tornado-like winds swept through the syndicate's Mission Bay compound. The team's sail loft and hospitality areas were destroyed. And the boat, *Young America*, suffered extensive damage.

As the team regrouped the morning after and began repairing the compound and *Young America*, PACT 95 president John Marshall looked upon the debris. "This will make us or break us."

The theme of the Citizen Cup became resiliency. All three teams refused to break.

PACT 95 not only rebounded from the tornado, but it also rebuilt *Young America* a second time after it was hit by a rogue wave in March.

The women held their own early with *America³*, then made a big jump forward after the new *Mighty Mary* finally arrived. Still, all was not smooth sailing for the Women's Team. The decision to bring Dave Dellenbaugh aboard the boat to replace J. J. Isler as tactician and starting helmsman on the morning of the first semifinal race triggered the biggest debate of the Citizen Cup.

No team, however, bounced back more often—or farther—than Conner's veteran band with *Stars & Stripes*. Team Dennis Conner even adopted the Bee Gees' upbeat "Stayin' Alive" as its official anthem.

On March 26, *Stars & Stripes* nearly sank. Three days later it was sailing again. Then, sent through to the finals by a last-minute compromise, *Stars & Stripes* rallied from a 4:08 deficit entering the last leg of the last race to win the right to defend the America's Cup.

ROUND ONE

The first match was tailor-made for the media covering the Women's Team. With PACT 95 given a couple extra days to complete the repairs to *Young America*, Conner's *Stars & Stripes* would be meeting the women in the series opener.

The defense syndicate leaders (below) join Citizen Watch Company of America president Laurence Grunstein (right) at the unveiling of the Citizen Cup trophy. From left are PACT 95 president John Marshall, Dennis Conner, and America³ boss Bill Koch.

FOLLOWING PAGES:

The Women's Team, easily identified by their sunflower hairbands, prepare to cross behind Stars & Stripes *while sailing* America³ *in the early round-robins. Little known before the trials began, helmsman—and that's the title she preferred—Leslie Egnot quickly emerged as one of the stars of America's Cup '95.*

The racing was close throughout the Citizen Cup. Midway up the first weather leg of their first meeting in the finals, Stars & Stripes *barely crossed in front of* Mighty Mary's *bow on port tack in perhaps the most critical crossing of the defense series. "Sometimes you have to go with your gut feeling," said* Stars & Stripes *helmsman Paul Cayard. "I thought we could make it . . . we did." The cross gave* Stars & Stripes *the lead. Team Dennis Conner sailed on to win the race—and the Citizen Cup.*

And the women won.

Handed the lead by a questionable foul call against Conner in the prestart maneuvering, the women deftly held Conner in check throughout the 18.55-mile race and crossed the finish line 76 seconds ahead of *Stars & Stripes*.

"It feels great," said Egnot, who, as helmsman, became an overnight celebrity. "I knew we could do it. We know it's just one race of a long series. But getting a win in our first race removes some of the pressure."

"The women sailed a good race," said Conner. "I didn't like the on-the-water umpires' call against us before the start, but that's a part of racing. Give the women credit. They beat us."

"This is an incredible feeling," said Isler. "I was really nervous out there . . . you know, that kind of pumped-up nervous. It was wonderfully exciting."

Unfortunately, the victory established a pattern for the women. In each of the first three round-robins, the women would win the first race of the series—then not win another. But the women sailed well on their older boat. *America³* could still hold its own against the next generation in the prestart maneuvering and upwind legs. It was downwind where *America³* usually lost ground to a combination of problems.

As the first round wore on, the focus moved from the women to *Stars & Stripes* and *Young America*.

The PACT 95 team had rebounded smartly from the near-catastrophe of January 4. *Young America* would sweep its three first-round races against the women and win two of three against *Stars & Stripes*. Designed by Bruce Nelson, *Young America* had the looks of a solid all-around performer.

Meantime, the winds of change were already stirring in the Team Dennis Conner compound. After his effort to refloat the Italian challenge had failed, Paul Cayard, the skipper of 1992 Louis Vuitton Cup winner *Il Moro di Venezia* joined Conner's crew. At first, his role was undefined. Cayard called himself the "instigator" and "free safety." "I move around on the boat to help wherever I can," he said. But as the first round moved along, Cayard was doing more of the steering on *Stars & Stripes* and Conner less.

ROUND TWO

The women opened the round by sailing *America³* to a hard-fought 14-second victory over *Young America* in the closest race of the trials to date. *Young America* skipper

America³ technician Alison Hamilton (above) keeps watch on the battery of Hewlett Packard computers the team used to monitor everything from boat performance to weather to sail inventories.

In the Whitbread Round The World Race, Dawn Riley (below) was skipper of the only all-women's crew. Aboard the America's Cup boat, however, crew captain Riley did a little of everything, including assist in sail takedowns.

Kevin Mahaney praised the work of *America³'s* braintrust—Egnot on the helm and Isler on tactics.

The unseasonable weather conditions played havoc with the second round of defense trials, eventually forcing the San Diego Yacht Club to shorten the series by a complete set.

Cayard continued to take on more and more responsibility on *Stars & Stripes*. In addition to handling the starts, he now was steering the boat on most of the upwind legs. The round ended with Team Dennis Conner tied for first in the standings with *Young America.*

Both the women and PACT 95 had problems on the downwind legs during the second round. "Everyone thought we'd have have problems in tacking duels," said *America³* grinder Stephanie Maxwell-Pierson. "We're more than holding our own going to weather." But setting and jibing the huge International America's Cup Class headsails downwind was a trickier proposition. And the women weren't alone. "Our headsail work leaves room for improvement," said Marshall.

ROUND THREE

The adjustments continued.

The women improved their downwind performance, although the old *America³* was having trouble keeping pace with its newer rivals. "There's not much more we can do to our boat while *Stars & Stripes* and *Young America* make improvements every round," said Egnot.

Nelson replaced Ken Read aboard *Young America* as strategist. Nelson answered two shortcomings of the PACT 95 crew. Many were new to the IACC class. And few had much experience sailing in San Diego's tricky conditions. In addition to being the designer of *Young America*, Nelson—a San Diego resident and world-class sailor—brought "local knowledge" to the crew.

"Bruce brings a lot to the boat," said Marshall. "As the designer, being aboard gives him the opportunity to analyze performance. And he's one of the game's best at spotting the weather here."

The defender races were much closer than the matches being sailed on the challenger course. Still, there was an edge that was missing. No boat was emerging as outstanding.

ROUND FOUR

Finally, the women received their new boat. Two days before the start of the fourth round-robin, Koch christened the distinctive sloop *Mighty Mary* after his mother.

PACT 95 president John Marshall forged a partnership between technology leaders including Ford and Science Applications International (SAIC) to assist naval architect Bruce Nelson (below) in the development of Young America (opposite). Nelson spent much of his time on the computer designing the boat that would defend the America's Cup.

The carbon-fiber North 3DL sails of Stars & Stripes *and* Young America *glisten in the sunlight as Team Dennis Conner crosses in front of the Mermaid during a round-robin race.*

Koch had waited as long as possible to build *Mighty Mary,* hoping the new boat would propel the Women's Team over the top. The new boat was fast. But the women had teething problems—particularly on the troublesome downwind legs.

Again, the weather took a toll on the defender trials, forcing cancellation of a set.

Young America finally broke its stalemate with *Stars & Stripes* and gained two bonus points for the semifinals by winning the round-robins. Despite a 1-3 record in the last round-robin, *Stars & Stripes* would take one bonus point into the semis.

Thus far, the defender trials had been relatively uneventful. All that was about to change.

THE SEMIFINALS

The semifinals of the Citizen Cup were perhaps the most eventful and contentious 17 days in the history of defense trials. Each of the three teams was involved in multiple controversies. In the end, an eleventh-hour compromise was struck sending all three boats to the finals.

At the time, the compromise seemed to sully the defender trials. As it turned out, the events of the semifinals led to a great conclusion of the Citizen Cup.

The problems began before the semifinals commenced. And they started again with *Young America.* On March 12 *Young America* was hit by a rogue, three-meter wave as it was being towed out through the entrance to Mission Bay. The impact damaged a 16-foot by four-foot section of the undersides between the bow and leading edge of the keel blade. For the second time in less than 10 weeks, the PACT 95 crew would work feverishly around the clock repairing its crippled boat.

Next, it was the women's turn. Hours before the first race of the semifinals, Koch called a team meeting. First, he handed out scarves to his then all-female crew. Then he dropped the bomb. Isler was coming off the boat. Dellenbaugh was going on. Henceforth, a man would handle the starts and call the tactics on *Mighty Mary.* It was no longer the "all-women's team," rather the "Women's Team."

Koch said it was a decision reached by the crew. "I have to eat a bit of crow now, but I don't think this is a big deal," said Koch. "After the last round, I met with three or four members of the crew who asked that we do something to improve the experience on the back of the boat. We went over the options, including asking ourselves why we are here—to win or to further the cause of women? The consensus was to win. I asked them

While being towed out through the entrance to Mission Bay on March 12, Young America *was hit by a series of rogue, three-meter waves that cracked a 16-foot section of the hull just forward of the keel blade. The PACT 95 crew worked around the clock for six days preparing the boat for its 8-1 run in the semifinals.*

FOLLOWING PAGES:

It never cracked, but the slightly flared hull of Stars & Stripes *was a design characteristic that many, including Conner, believed limited the boat's potential.*

Young America *(top)* and Stars & Stripes *circle looking for an opening during a prestart exchange. Team Dennis Conner's Paul Cayard, the most experienced of the three defense helmsmen, won more than his share of starts with* Stars & Stripes.

who they would choose to be tactician on the boat. They made their choice and I went with it."

The move sent shockwaves through the compounds . . . and far beyond.

Said Mahaney: "I'm somewhat surprised. I thought they were doing a nice job tactically. J. J. was doing a good job placing the boat on the water." Said *Stars & Stripes* tactician Tom Whidden: "No way J. J.'s the biggest problem they have. We don't understand the change. They have come all this way and then do that. Why? We actually thought they were gaining some momentum."

Then the racing began.

On March 26, the hastily repaired *Young America*—seeking a fourth straight win—was narrowly ahead of *Stars & Stripes* midway up the second weather leg. Suddenly, *Stars & Stripes* dropped its sails and sat dead in the water. The crew hustled about the deck. The first indication of the degree of trouble came when a flotation and marker buoy was quickly raised to the top of the mast and the crew began donning life jackets. *Stars & Stripes* was in danger of sinking.

The keel had all but fallen off the boat. Pumps were rushed aboard and flotation bags were jammed into the hole between the bottom of the hull and the top of the keel. "I'm not joking when I say I thought we might sink," said helmsman Paul Cayard.

Sink or not, it appeared *Stars & Stripes's* run might be over. The crew worked around the clock repairing the separated keel with the boat's original keel. Miraculously, *Stars & Stripes* was back on the race course within 48 hours. More amazing, the rebuilt boat beat *Mighty Mary* by 1:31.

Next, the protests flew. *America³* would file a total of 10 against *Stars & Stripes* and the San Diego Yacht Club Defense Committee claiming the repairs made to *Stars & Stripes* were illegal. Damaged boats could be repaired during a round, but not modified. Because the switched keels were not identical, *America³* claimed the repairs were modifications. *Young America* joined *America³*'s protest.

The international jury quickly ruled there was a small discrepancy on the keel change, vacated *Stars & Stripes's* victory over *Mighty Mary*, ordered a small fix in *Stars & Stripes's* new keel and called for the semifinals to resume. *America³* appealed the jury's ruling. Then it came to light that *Young America* might also have made a small modification during the no-change period. Team Dennis Conner protested.

On the water, *Mighty Mary* won three races and was ahead of *Stars & Stripes* going into the final day of the semifinals. *Stars & Stripes* defeated *Mighty Mary* by 4:49 in light

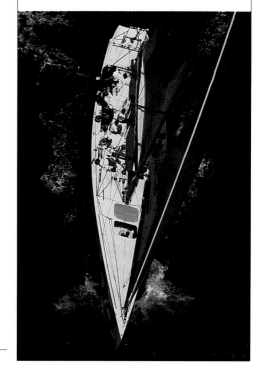

Bruce Nelson's "long and narrow" Young America (below) was designed to slice through San Diego's rough seas with the minimum of resistance.

winds to force a one-race sail-off to see which would advance to the finals opposite *Young America.*

The forecast for the April 4 showdown called for continuing light winds, which would favor *Stars &* *Stripes.* Early in the morning of the sail-off, America³ initiated talks regarding a compromise that would send all three defense candidates to the finals. The deal was struck just before the boats headed out for the final race.

"Everything from sponsors to weather forecasts was considered in the negotiations," said America³ president Vince Moeyersoms. "For the best of everyone concerned, we agreed that no one should be eliminated at this stage."

The compromise was widely criticized.

Many observers couldn't understand why PACT 95—which was assured a spot in the finals—would agree to a three-way sail-off . . . even if the deal did give them a repeat of the two bonus wins that carried *Young America* successfully through the semifinals. "The compromise offers us some security," said Marshall. "We ran all the options through the SAIC computer and this compromise offered us the best deal."

There was one remaining problem with the compromise. No one told the mostly women's crew on *Mighty Mary.* When they defeated *Stars & Stripes* by a whopping 5:59, the women believed they had knocked Conner out of the America's Cup. "Before we went into the race, we thought there was no deal left," said Egnot. "We went in thinking 'do or die.' When we finished, I've never seen such happy people. We excelled today under the highest of pressure. It was a real disappointment when we heard what had happened."

THE FINALS

Even the challengers were stunned by the compromise.

"You don't do anything to help Dennis," said *oneAustralia* helmsman Rod Davis. "If you've got Dennis Conner down, you keep him down. You don't put him back in the game. I can see it now . . . Dennis coming back and winning the defense finals. It can happen."

It did.

When the spray settled, Conner's *Stars & Stripes* emerged as the champion of the Citizen Cup. Implausible, yes. But it happened. And that's not the half of it.

Stars & Stripes trailed the women by 4:08 starting the last leg of the last race of the trials. Were *Stars & Stripes* to win the race, Team Dennis Conner would defend the America's Cup. If *Mighty Mary* won, the Women's Team would meet *Young America* the

Only America³ *boss Bill Koch (below) was happy on* Mighty Mary *the afternoon of April 4. The women thought they had knocked Conner's* Stars & Stripes *out of the trials with a lopsided victory in the last race of the semifinals. But the crew wasn't told of the last-minute compromise that sent all three defenders to the finals.*

Through the first three round-robins the women's team was handicapped, having to sail the older America³ *until* Mighty Mary *(opposite) arrived.*

FOLLOWING PAGES:

As port trimmer Grant Spanhake gauges the trim of the genoa, the PACT 95 after-guard of mainsheet trimmer Andreas Josenhans (white cap, left), navigator Robert Hopkins (blue sweater at pedestal), skipper Kevin Mahaney (on wheel), and tactician John Kostecki analyze Young America's *performance.*

*A*pril 9 was a significant day in America's Cup '95. An agreement between the challengers and defenders led to the first public unveiling of America's Cup keels since Australia II went under wraps to hide its controversial winged keel in 1983. The biggest surprise of the day-long unveilings was the amount of similarities between the boats. Mighty Mary's huge rudder drew oohs and ahhs. But there were no tandems or forward canards. Young America (above) attracted a bevy of photographers, who made the most of the first opportunity to capture artist Roy Lichtenstein's entire mermaid graphic.

next afternoon to determine the defender.

ESPN already was flashing the starting time for the *Young America/Mighty Mary* sail-off on the screen. No boat ever had come back from a 4:08 deficit on the last leg.

Stars & Stripes did . . . and then some. *Stars & Stripes* won by 52 seconds—meaning Conner's boat picked up five minutes on the three-mile run to the gun.

"I've had my share of comebacks," Conner said. "But this is by far the most amazing yet."

He was talking about the final race. But he could have meant the entire final round. Remember, *Stars & Stripes* spotted *Young America* two wins and the women one coming into the finals, which would pit each defense candidate against its rivals four times for a total of eight races. And *Stars & Stripes* not only was considered the slowest of the three defenders, it still was wounded from its dekeeling in the semifinals.

In the shortened, one-week break between the end of the weather-extended semifinals and the start of the finals, the *Stars & Stripes* crew gave its campaigner yet another makeover. A wedge was taken out of the hull at the deck to slightly extend the waterline. Still, *Stars & Stripes* was the only defender with a flared hull. Both *Young America* and *Mighty Mary* were slab-sided. "I'm no expert on design," said Conner, "but my instincts tell me we're off."

When the finals started, *Stars & Stripes* was on. It was *Young America*, which had won 21 of its 28 races through the semifinals, that was suddenly off.

Mighty Mary defeated *Young America* in the opener of the Citizen Cup finals. Then *Stars & Stripes*, which had lost six straight matches to the PACT 95 crew, beat both *Young America* and *Mighty Mary*—quickly knotting the finals at two wins apiece. *Young America* had made tactical errors in both of its losses. Now it made a configuration change, adding small wings—called "Nelsons" for their designer—to the rudder.

Young America defeated *Mighty Mary*, but again lost to *Stars & Stripes*. The women rebounded to stop Conner's three-race winning streak. At the midpoint of the finals, all three boats had three wins.

Then the pendulum swung dramatically in *Stars & Stripes's* favor. Conner's crew won both its matches in the third of four sets to improve its record to 5-1.

To win the Citizen Cup, all *Stars & Stripes* needed to do was win one race against either *Young America* or *Mighty Mary* in the final set. Suddenly, PACT 95 and America³ sensed an urgent need to cooperate. The teams began testing together. They swapped weather information. America³ boss Moeyersoms was spotted on the PACT 95 tender. Were both

*S*an Diego Yacht Club's defense committee (below) oversaw several tough decisions, including the compromise that sent all three boats to the finals and Conner's switch to Young America *for the* America's Cup. *From left, wearing Helly Hansen jackets, are Sandy Purdon, Art De Fever, chairman G. Wytie Cable and Bill Packer. Helly Hansen also supplied foul weather gear for the entire America's Cup Race Management team.*

*D*ays after almost losing its keel, the hastily repaired Stars & Stripes *returned to the races—and won. But the rekeeling and following victory over* Mighty Mary *triggered a rash of protests that eventually led to the controversial com-* *promise that sent all three defenders to the finals. "When the keel came off, I really thought we could sink," said helmsman Paul Cayard. "This crew just refuses to quit," said Conner.*

to defeat *Stars & Stripes* in the last set, *Mighty Mary* and *Young America* would meet in a one-race sail-off to choose the defender. That would be dealt with later. The immediate problem was *Stars & Stripes*.

Conner was upset. He believed the cooperation between his enemies was unethical if not illegal. "You are not allowed to win by anything other than your own skills," argued Conner. Countered Moeyersoms: "We're trying to have a positive influence on our destiny. We are free to tune up against whomever we choose."

The plan seemed to be working. After slicing off the rudder wings, *Young America* defeated *Stars & Stripes* by 52 seconds. And after five of six legs of the last race in the series, *Mighty Mary* had pulled away to a 4:08 lead; the women's margin over *Stars & Stripes* was more than 40 boat lengths.

As *Stars & Stripes* rounded the last mark and set sail for the right side of the course, Conner turned to Whidden—his closest aide for six campaigns spanning 15 years—and said: "If we get ourselves out of this one, it's going to be a miracle comeback."

That it was. The Citizen Cup would take one last incredible twist. As Isler's replacement, Dellenbaugh made the tactical decisions aboard *Mighty Mary*. Rounding the last mark, he elected to follow the shortest path to the finish rather than place *Mighty Mary* between the finish and *Stars & Stripes* in a classic covering position.

Off to the left corner of the course, *Mighty Mary* ran low on wind as *Stars & Stripes* picked up a fresher breeze on the right and rode it down toward the women. The boats swapped jibes. Again, the women's recurring problem with downwind sail trim caused them to lose more ground. Then the women sailed into a hole. *Stars & Stripes* broke though into the lead. Not even a shredded spinnaker could stop Conner's team. Nearing the finish line, Cayard did an excellent job positioning *Stars & Stripes* between the finish and *Mighty Mary*.

"Is that the race of all time, or is that the race of all time?" said Cayard. "We never ever gave up. I don't know why, but we never gave up. For some reason, as we rounded the last mark, I had a feeling we were still in the race. I don't know why. I just had a feeling."

Conner was going to his sixth America's Cup. And the historic first women's campaign had ended.

"I thought our team did a great job," said Egnot. "It's tough to lose like we did today. We probably should have jibed earlier and covered. Who would have known?"

"We lost because we didn't cover," said Koch. "What do they say? Pigs get fat, hogs get slaughtered."

Conner had won the right to defend the America's Cup. Next he went looking for a boat up to the task.

With the Citizen Cup in one hand and the American flag in the other, Dennis Conner celebrates his miracle comeback.

FOLLOWING PAGES:

Team Dennis Conner partied briefly but then quickly opened negotiations with PACT 95 to secure Young America *for the America's Cup defense.*

THE AMERICA'S CUP

THE XXIXTH DEFENSE

As it turned out, it didn't matter. Team New Zealand's *Black Magic* could have raced all three defenders at once—à la *Cambria* in 1870—and probably have won the America's Cup with ease.

But what is the America's Cup without a little intrigue. Yes, the most interesting aspect of the actual defense was Team Dennis Conner's last-minute boat switch.

Knowing he had been fortunate to win the right to defend with *Stars & Stripes,* Conner moved quickly after the conclusion of the Citizen Cup defender finals to put a faster hull under his capable crew.

Conner parked *Stars & Stripes* and elected to sail PACT 95's vanquished *Young America* against *Black Magic* in the America's Cup.

The switch was perfectly legal. The opening was in a loophole clause of the mutual consent item establishing a common declaration date for defenders and challengers alike.

Originally, the common declaration date was seen as a victory for the challengers, who in past multinational America's Cup challenges had to name their respective boats before the trials began while the defenders could wait until the morning of the first America's Cup race to choose their weapon.

In 1995, each challenging syndicate didn't have to name its boat until April 9—the eve of the challenger and defense finals and the day the surviving contenders unveiled their keels for all to see.

The common declaration date had been granted

to the challengers as a tradeoff for the unveiling ceremony—which organizers of America's Cup '95 justifiably believed was critical to improving the general public's interest in the event.

When the agreement was signed, it was clear that each challenger would be limited to the boat unveiled on April 9. It was assumed that each defender would be, too.

But nothing can be assumed in the America's Cup. Every clause in every paragraph is examined ad nauseam. As it turned out, the defenders were limited only to the boats unveiled on April 9. The common declaration agreement didn't address who might be sailing which boat. And because the defenders had struck the last-minute compromise sending all three candidates to the defense finals, there were three boats in the mix rather than two.

Team New Zealand had committed itself to NZL-32. But the defenders were free to choose among *Stars & Stripes, Young America,* or *Mighty Mary.*

The possibility of a boat switch didn't catch Team New Zealand by surprise. It was the challenger's rules advisor, Sean Reeves, who first noticed the opening during the earliest days of the trials.

At first, the Challenger of Record Committee asked the San Diego Yacht Club to close the loophole as a voluntary "gesture of good faith." San Diego Yacht Club said no.

The CORC then took the dispute to the three-member Trustees' Committee, which ruled in San Diego Yacht Club's favor.

*H*elmsman Paul Cayard and members of the Stars & Stripes *crew inspect the deck layout of* Young America *moments after Dennis Conner acquired the PACT 95 boat to defend the America's Cup.*

Conner's crew wasted little time getting Young America *(opposite) on the water for practice.*

The decision angered the challengers. Ernie Taylor turned in his guest card at the San Diego Yacht Club over the ruling.

Still, it didn't look as though anything would come of the ruling . . . until *Young America* lost its competitive edge in the defense finals and Conner's team emerged as the defender.

No question that *Stars & Stripes* was the slowest of the three defense candidates. Many experts believed Conner's entry was also one of the slowest boats in the combined challenger/defender fleet.

No problem. As soon as his team won the right to defend, Conner decided to invoke the "switching clause." *Stars & Stripes* was out. *Young America* was in.

Naturally, the switch upset Team New Zealand. The challengers formally appealed the switch to the Trustees' Committee. The appeal was denied. Team New Zealand syndicate director Peter Blake then fired a verbal broadside at the switch—accusing San Diego Yacht Club and Conner of "bending the rules."

"Everyone came here expecting a level playing field under the new rules for the America's Cup," said Blake. "All that has happened is that the defender . . . reverted to its

Black Magic *bowman Dean Phipps looks for an opening behind the committee boat after* Young America *successfully pushed the* challenger *outside the starting area before the second race.* Black Magic *skipper Russell Coutts made a quick recovery, however, and sailed to victory.*

old ways and has wound up emasculating the Mutual Consent items, which were to be the cornerstone of the new America's Cup that everyone wanted. The mix and match of syndicate and boat, which the Trustees have now surprisingly permitted, cuts right across many of the new measures introduced to improve the event."

Something was missing, however, from Team New Zealand's response to the boat switch.

The Kiwis were upset, but not angered. It had been said that New Zealand's three previous America's Cup ventures collapsed when the Kiwis took their eyes off the prize and became irrational about secondary topics.

"Glassgate" in 1987 preceeded the *Stars & Stripes* rout of *Kiwi Magic* in the challenger finals. Everyone wishes to forget the court wranglings involved in the 1988 "Big Boat" fiasco. And then there was "Bowspritgate" in 1992.

Hours after winning a race that apparently gave New Zealand a 4-1 lead over *Il Moro di Venezia* in the best 5-of-9 challenger finals, the Italians won a protest regarding New Zealand's use of its controversial bowsprit. The protest committee removed the fourth win from the books. Paul Cayard then skippered *Il Moro di Venezia* to four straight close wins to eliminate the Kiwis 5-3.

"That was a bitter-tasting defeat," said grinder Andrew Taylor, the only member of Team New Zealand to have sailed on all four of New Zealand's America's Cup bids.

"But we have learned our lessons. We have come a long way since Australia in 1987 . . . even from 1992. Our past campaigns were run by managers. This campaign is structured more from the needs and the thoughts of the sailing team. Control and direction comes from the boat."

In past challenges, New Zealand might not have been able to put the *Young America*-for-*Stars & Stripes* switch behind it. This time, Blake made his statement for the team and moved on.

As the America's Cup approached, the Team New Zealand crew kept a low profile. They could be seen smiling as they entered and departed their America's Cup Harbor base. But they said little for public consumption.

"We've stayed squeaky clean this time," said Taylor. "This is a vicious game. We didn't want to get into a position where outside things could bother us like they did before."

And they didn't. Not even the first boat switch in America's Cup history could rattle these Kiwis.

After all, here was the opportunity to exorcise all the ghosts of America's Cups past.

San Diego Yacht Club. Conner. Cayard. All sitting in one boat—*Young America.*

One of the 31 race course patrol boats (below) supplied by Bayliner glides past Team New Zealand's spectator boat during the America's Cup. The 29th defense depended upon a cadre of volunteers for everything from traffic control to race committee assistance.

FOLLOWING PAGES:

An umpire boat follows the action in the background as Black Magic *rounds a leeward mark as the trailing* Young America *still sails downwind.*

*T*he first downwind leg of the America's Cup offered a glimmer of hope to the defenders. Down by 31 seconds at the top mark, Young America *closed on the run and almost pulled even before losing ground on a bad jibe near the leeward mark.* Black Magic *led by 12 seconds at the mark—the closest of 25 roundings during the five races.*

"A lot of people on this team have scores to settle with the defenders," said a smiling Warwick Fleury, *Black Magic's* mainsheet trimmer. "They've beaten all of us at this game at some time in one way or another."

Even Doug Peterson, who co-designed the NZL-32 and NZL-38 hulls with New Zealand native Laurie Davidson had some unfinished business with Team Dennis Conner.

Peterson worked with America[3] in 1992 and offered his services to Conner for the 1995 campaign. But he was turned down. "Dennis pretty much told me he didn't need a designer," said Peterson.

The week before the May 6 opener of the first 5-of-9 America's Cup was a sharp study in contrasts.

Conner's team—which was renamed Team Stars & Stripes from Team Dennis Conner to maintain some identity with the syndicate's decade-old Stars & Stripes theme —worked long hours in a desperate attempt to learn its new boat.

Black Magic's final winning margins were the widest in 21 years, but the first weather legs typically produced a number of close stern-to-bow crosses like this first-race meeting (below).

"*Young America* and *Stars & Stripes* aren't very similar," said Cayard. "Some of the differences are easy adjustments. But some are much more difficult. *Young America* had a considerably different deck organization. There are some winches in different places and the leads are different. And there's the feel of the boat. Maybe the toughest adjustments to make are the subtle ones . . . learning the feel of when you're performing well and when you're not up to speed."

That was a problem inside a problem.

As Team Stars & Stripes worked overtime to get up to speed, Conner knew Team New Zealand had *Black Magic* at near maximum performance levels.

Conner's crew sailed and sailed. The *Black Magic* crew sailed . . . and played golf. "We've pretty much done all we can do," said Blake. "I think it is just important now to be mentally relaxed. We're ready, but relaxed.

"I don't think we can get our boat moving any faster. This is the best shot we'll ever have."

Conner's crew was neither relaxed nor ready.

In the days before the America's Cup, attention turned to the two boats. When the semifinalists were unveiled on April 9, everyone noted the striking similarities between *Young America* and *Black Magic*.

"The extremely different paint jobs make the boats look different," said *Young America* lead designer Bruce Nelson. *Young America* had the Roy Lichtenstein graphic of the mermaid while *Black Magic* was distinctly black.

But if both hulls were white?

"The mermaid on *Young America* is in the nature of camouflage and our black hull tends to play tricks with the eyes," said Team New Zealand co-designer Laurie Davidson.

"I think there are some basic similarities between the two boats," said Peterson. "I think the two design teams probably followed the same path and came to much the same conclusions."

It made sense that the design teams were on parallel paths. Both Nelson and Peterson are based in San Diego and have considerable working knowledge of the vagaries of San Diego's weather. Indeed, *Young America's* performance improved when Nelson came aboard the boat as strategist during the round-robins.

*Y*es, the Kiwis have a sense of humor. The flames painted on the nose of the Black Magic *keel bulb (below) made it look more like a '32 roadster than a high-tech International America's Cup Class appendage.*

The most notable artistic achievement of the 1995 America's Cup was Roy Lichtenstein's hull-length mermaid graphic on Young America *(opposite). After the January 4 tornado, PACT 95 nicknamed their mermaid "Dorothy."*

"I know Doug and I share the same ideas about what makes a boat good," said Davidson. "And I imagine Nelson is on the same page."

But if the boats were similar, there were also striking differences—both in the subtleties and components of design.

Nelson's team spent much of its time working on computers. Peterson and Davidson spent far less time on computers and more time working with models in a towing basin.

Each side wished it had more time working in the other's arena. Nelson's budget restricted the team's model testing. Peterson and Davidson didn't have the computer tools available to Nelson.

"Both systems work if done correctly," said Davidson. "But a computer can't design. Computers verify. Designers design."

And on the eve of the first races, Peterson let the secret slip out. Team New Zealand had more than two designers. It had a team.

"Beyond that," said Peterson. "We involved everyone in the design of the *Black Magics*." Everyone?

"Everyone. This is a totally integrated program," said Peterson. "The shape of the hull is not the reason we're winning. Just like it's not the sails or the rig or the crew or the appendages . . . by themselves. It's not any one thing. It's the package. And everyone had a hand in the package.

"When we were designing the boat, we'd lay the plans out on the table. Members of the crew were invited to come in at any time they wanted to look at what we were doing and make suggestions.

"It was their boat and their work station. It had to work for them. And the only way

you can make that happen to everyone's satisfaction is to involve everyone in everything."

The *Black Magic* design program was managed by Tom Schnackenberg, an expert in sail design and a man whom Conner believes is "maybe the top brain in sailing."

"The secret is boring," said Schnackenberg. "It's the teamwork. It sounds obvious. It is obvious. But it's not easy. Our success was the sum of the parts added up.

"We won because everything we put into the boat works together. We didn't view the hulls, the sails, and the crew separately. We looked at everything as a unit. The boat."

Black Magic.

RACE ONE: *Black Magic* BY 2:45

The morning of May 6 saw the latest Pacific storm sweep through San Diego, leaving a sloppy sea and shifty eight- to 13-knot winds. The conditions halved the expected spectator fleet to 500 boats.

As he did in the 1992 America's Cup while skippering *Il Moro di Venezia*, *Young America* helmsman Paul Cayard tried to engage *Black Magic* in a prestart fight. Russell Coutts didn't bite.

On the first two laps, the fortunes of the antagonists seemed to rise and fall with the shifts. *Black Magic* got the first shift and turned it into a quick lead. But *Black Magic* barely crossed *Young America* two-thirds of the way up the first weather leg and led by 12 seconds at the end of the first run. *Black Magic* padded its lead by 70 seconds on the second lap.

Then came the first hint of disaster for the defenders.

At the start of the third beat, *Black Magic* was below *Young America* as the pair started a long drag race to the right. By the time *Young America* tacked, *Black Magic* had sailed across the defender's bow—doubling the lead on the leg.

Black Magic became the first non-American challenger to win the opening race since *Endeavour* in 1934.

"We're excited about winning," said tactician Brad Butterworth. "But these were some of the hardest waves we've dealt with."

"Today wasn't an easy day to sail a first race in a new boat," said Cayard. "You really had to know your boat to sail well today. They did."

RACE TWO: *Black Magic* BY 4:14

The second race, sailed on May 8, was one for the record books.

Dennis Conner's crew hustles on Young America's *foredeck as the gennaker threatens to go over the bow as the defender nears a leeward mark trailing* Black Magic.

The margin of victory was the greatest by a challenger since *Livonia* defeated *Columbia* by 15:10 seconds in 1871. Excluding the 1988 catamaran debacle, the margin was the greatest of any America's Cup race dating back to *Courageous's* series-clinching victory over *Southern Cross* in 1974.

And the conditions—eight-knot winds and four-foot seas—were what *Young America* was designed to excel in.

"We're not used to that kind of a stomping," admitted Bill Trenkle, who has sailed with Conner for 15 years. "That was hard on our guys."

"We basically out-sailed them big-time today," said *Black Magic* co-designer Doug Peterson. "But this was also boat speed."

Cayard reluctantly agreed: "On the first run, I thought they were pulling away from us because of the sail they had up. Maybe they're just faster. One thing is clear, they can sail higher than we can."

And to think Cayard won the start. He buried *Black Magic* behind the committee boat. Coutts made a nice last-second recovery just to get back to the starting line.

But before the words "Nice start, Paul," cleared *Young America* skipper Dennis Conner's lips, *Black Magic* led.

"We had one of the finest starts I've ever seen and *Black Magic* answered with an unbelieveable gain," said *Young America* crewman Josh Belsky. "This is not good."

RACE THREE: *Black Magic* BY 1:51

Cayard came out swinging on May 9. He tried to force *Black Magic* over the starting line early. Once again, Coutts adroitly sailed himself out of the trap with an even start.

This time, however, *Young America* got the race's first shift on the left side of the course. The defenders might have led. We'll never know for sure.

When *Young America* tacked to consolidate its possible advantage, Coutts kept *Black Magic* heading out to the right. In a span of three minutes and one small shift, *Black Magic* had the necessary advantage to cross ahead of *Young America*. The defenders hung on throughout the first beat. Twice *Young America's* bow passed just behind *Black Magic's* transom during a tacking duel. Once it appeared *Young America* might break through a *Black Magic* slam dunk.

But the Kiwis refused to buckle under pressure. Then *Black Magic* sailed away as the winds grew steadily from seven to 14 knots.

Black Magic *only once saw this scene—the transom of* Young America. *Here, helmsman Paul Cayard and his crew tune up before a start.*

FOLLOWING PAGES:

Sail changes on Black Magic *were almost a work of art. The spinnaker is already up and drawing as the* Black Magic *crew drops the genoa.*

"I didn't think the series would be like this," said Butterworth. "We're really sailing well and we seem to have an edge in boats."

A mid-race give-and-take between Cayard and *Young America* tactician Tom Whidden said it all. Cayard: "They're not even covering us anymore." Whidden: "I don't even think they're looking back."

"When we get *Black Magic* into a match-racing situation, our crew does a good job," said Conner. "But match racing is not their game. When we engage, they just break it off, use their boat speed, and sail away."

RACE FOUR: *Black Magic* BY 3:37

After races on consecutive days, the day off between races three and four allowed the *Young America* crew to test some just-arrived sails.

"The next race will decide if we have any chance at all," said Cayard. On May 11, the defenders got their answer. It was a resounding NO.

However, *Young America* did lead. Twice on the first weather leg, Cayard used the starboard tacking advantage to pass two boat lengths in front of *Black Magic*. A solid start and a pair of right-hand shifts had put the defenders in front.

Then, *Black Magic* hit a 15-degree shift out on the left side of the course. In an eight-minute span, *Black Magic* went from two lengths behind to eight lengths ahead. The Kiwis's lead at the first mark was 1:09—their largest yet by 30 seconds.

The rout was on.

"I've been in some uphill battles in my life," said Cayard. "But I've never before been in a race where I really felt I had so little control over the outcome. It's the largest discrepancy in boat speed that I've personally [seen].

"I don't feel like I'm in a sailboat race. We get a shift and fight for a two-length lead. They get a shift and it's 10 lengths. And it's the same strength shift."

"It's unbelievable how easy this has been," said *Black Magic* strategist Murray Jones.

Whidden agreed: "I never guessed there would be this kind of discrepancy. We never imagined the entire defense program was so far off pace. I'm surprised."

RACE FIVE: *Black Magic* BY 1:50

The conditions were perfect for a just conclusion of America's Cup '95.

The seas were running to eight feet and the winds were swinging 20 degrees in

The closest weather mark rounding of the America's Cup. Black Magic's *chute begins to fill after rounding the first mark of the third race with a 20-second lead over* Young America *(below).*

In an oft-repeated scene, Black Magic *crosses ahead of* Young America *going to weather (opposite).*

To the victor goes the bubbly. Black Magic mainsheet caddie Peter Blake—who also happened to be the head of the Team New Zealand syndicate—sprays members of the Black Magic crew with a demijohn of Moët following the challenger's 5-0 sweep.

either direction and rising and falling between six and 10 knots.

The boats split tacks coming off the line with Cayard and *Young America* at the committee boat. *Young America* got the first shift. *Black Magic* got the second. When *Young America* got the next shift, it tacked. Coming in on port, *Black Magic* couldn't cross ahead and it appeared *Young America* had the narrowest of leads.

But the next shift went left. Game, set, and match. Thirteen minutes later, *Black Magic* had a four-length lead.

Unlike the first four races, this wasn't a rout. Both teams were having mechanical problems. The jib halyard broke on both boats and *Young America* lost four lengths while sailing without a headsail. No matter.

Black Magic pulled steadily and slowly away. The America's Cup was New Zealand's. The Slaughter on The Water was complete. "Did we slaughter these guys or what?" asked a jubilant Doug Peterson. "We were dominating. Other teams are going to have a hard time figuring out how we did it." But it wouldn't be difficult to figure out what *Black Magic* did. The numbers will be there for eternity . . . a testament to superiority.

During the America's Cup, *Black Magic* led at all 30 marks and lost time to *Young America* on only four legs—two of those being the final run to the finish. Again excluding the catamaran defense, *Black Magic's* average margin of victory—2:52—was the greatest since the *Courageous* rout of *Southern Cross* in 1974.

The 5-0 sweep of *Young America* capped an amazing four-month campaign that saw *Black Magic* post a 42-1 mark on the water. The average margin of victory: 3:06.

Not once in 43 races was *Black Magic* passed when ahead. Of course, the Kiwis didn't afford the opposition many opportunities. *Black Magic* led at 93 percent of the marks thoughout the campaign and gained time on 77 percent of its legs.

"From day one to the last run, from the top of the program to the bottom, we worked for excellence," concluded syndicate head Peter Blake. "We wanted to build a program that would not only win the America's Cup, but one that would do it proudly for New Zealand."

As he held the America's Cup for the first time, Brad Butterworth did a double-clutch on his emotions. "I don't know the words to say how fantastic this feels."

"I know all of New Zealand is celebrating," said Blake. "But I don't think it's really sunk in what we've done." For Team New Zealand didn't just win the America's Cup. The *Black Magic* crew rewrote the standards against which all future endeavors will be judged. "Top that," said Doug Peterson.

"Our congratulations to New Zealand," said America's Cup '95 chairman Frank Hope. "Our wish is that the contestants and the community will look back favorably upon the event.

*D*ennis Conner, with his wife Daintry, gives a "thumbs up" to the Black Magic *crew. "The America's Cup will have a good life in New Zealand," said the skipper responsible for bringing it to San Diego.*

FOLLOWING PAGES:

Black Magic *skipper Russell Coutts waves the New Zealand flag as members of Team New Zealand's extended family enjoy the victory celebration at the San Diego Yacht Club.*

"MISSION ACCOMPLISHED!"
THE KIWI CELEBRATION

It became a ritual at the Team New Zealand compound.

Put a new roll of paper in the fax machine every night. Put a new roll of paper in the fax machine every morning.

"The flood of calls come in overnight here," explained Team New Zealand syndicate director Peter Blake. "The last thing people do back home each night is send us a fax."

In this age of communications, one of the best ways to judge the pulse of an endeavor is the fax machine.

And the *Black Magic* crew never had to look very far to see how their efforts were being received 19 time zones and 6,500 miles from home.

Faxes poured in daily from Auckland to Christchurch and points between . . . from fishermen and farmers, from students and teachers.

Plus, the mail. Bags of it daily. An entire wall of the Team New Zealand offices was quickly dedicated to the drawings of young New Zealand artists. Then two walls . . . and office windows.

Each victory brought another flood of well wishes. And the numbers grew exponentially.

"I'm getting a little afraid about winning this thing," *Black Magic* tactician Brad Butterworth said one morning while stepping over the latest pile of congratulatory greetings. "The celebration back home could kill us."

Butterworth was joking. After all, it was the first week of April. The Louis Vuitton Cup Finals hadn't even begun. The Kiwis were just getting ready for the big push.

*A*s New Zealand prime minister Jim Bolger said: "Mission accomplished." The leadership team of Black Magic *skipper Russell Coutts (left), Team New Zealand syndicate director* Peter Blake (behind the America's Cup) and Royal New Zealand Yacht Squadron commodore Peter Hay (right) hold the America's Cup aloft during the formal awards ceremony at the San Diego Yacht Club.

Perhaps it was the Red Socks Caper that tuned the rest of the world into what was going on in New Zealand. Blake was also a working member of the *Black Magic* crew. Aboard the boat, he wore red socks. Call it superstition. "The red socks would make it easier for them to find me should I need to be plucked from the water," joked Blake.

The red socks do stand out. So much so that they took on celebrity status back in New Zealand. So much so that they became a promotion.

A New Zealand company decided to market "Peter Blake's Red Socks" at $10 a pair. Half of each sale would go directly to Team New Zealand. Nice little promotion. They made 20,000. Sold out. They made another 20,000. Sold out. One-hundred-thousand socks. Gone in five days.

"Ahhh, it's getting a little crazy," said Blake. A little?

Lotto was one of Team New Zealand's sponsors. Lotto activity reportedly went up 20 percent. Steinlager was another sponsor. Worldwide sales soared 35 percent.

As for TVNZ, the daily race coverage dominated the market . . . which caused a major problem in New Zealand.

New Zealand is five hours behind and a day ahead of San Diego. Races that began at 1 p.m. Saturday off Point Loma were aired live on New Zealand television at 8 a.m. Sunday. Sunday races in San Diego were sailed on Monday in New Zealand.

Church attendance took a beating. Some services around the country were rescheduled for the afternoon. And some businesses didn't open until noon so that employees and customers could view the races.

America's Cup mania grew as *Black Magic* eliminated *oneAustralia* in the finals of the Louis Vuitton Cup.

The stage was set. The island nation of 3.4 million people and 50 million sheep braced itself. Auckland, which prides itself as "The City of Sails," prepared to party.

Instead, an eerie silence fell over New Zealand.

The opening race drew an 85 share on TV New Zealand on Sunday morning, May 7. And there was little dropoff in the races that began early in the morning of the following Tuesday and Wednesday.

"At a quarter past eight, you could fire a shotgun down the streets of Wellington and not hit a soul," said Islay McLeod, a public relations consultant.

It was during the second race that district court judge Stephen Erber impaneled a jury at Greymouth. Before the jury retired to pick a foreman, Erber announced: "New

*H*ome at last. Skipper Russell Coutts and syndicate head Peter Blake display the America's Cup at the Auckland airport moments after arriving home on an Air New Zealand flight from San Diego.

*M*ore than 300,000 Kiwis turned out for the welcome home parade through the downtown streets of the Auckland. The crowd was so thick that the motorcade often slowed to a crawl. Auckland had to wait a week to celebrate, as Team New Zealand visited New York City and Washington, D.C., before closing its San Diego compound and flying home.

Zealand is leading by two minutes and 28 seconds at the fourth mark." Just before the first witness was called in the arson case, Erber told the jury, "We are now leading by four and a half minutes at the fifth mark."

Those New Zealanders who could book flights for San Diego did. Local tourist officials estimated that at least 5,000 New Zealanders were in San Diego during the America's Cup.

Robi Quilter went the opposite direction, however. Throughout the trials, the wife of *Black Magic* backup navigator Mike Quilter had lived in San Diego. But just before the America's Cup, Mrs. Quilter flew home. Why?

"I wanted to be part of the atmosphere in New Zealand," she explained. "I just knew it would be crazy. People truly believe down here that if you don't wear red socks, you could cause *Black Magic* to lose. Besides, I love our wonderfully biased TV-New Zealand coverage."

Biased and comprehensive.

On the last day of the America's Cup, the prerace program went on at 7 a.m. in New Zealand and continued until eight that night—13 hours that included the race, the dockside celebration at the San Diego Yacht Club, and the party in the Team New Zealand compound.

The coverage drew a record 92 share in New Zealand. At its peak, more than five of every seven New Zealanders were tuned into the fifth and final victory. At 8 p.m., the reruns and party scenes were still attracting three of every five viewers.

Talk show lines jammed with America's Cup calls. "I've never seen a topic as hot as this one and it's nothing but good," said Leighton Smith, host of the nation's top-rated morning talk show. "I've had farmers in the field who have a cellular phone but no radio call me for updates."

All that was left was for the America's Cup to go to its new home. The America's Cup landed in Auckland on Wednesday, May 24. There followed a parade the likes of which Auckland has never before seen. More than 300,000 greeted the America's Cup and its champions. Then another 200,000 at Wellington. Ditto for Christchurch.

"Little ol' New Zealand has just won the America's Cup," said Blake. "That's pretty damn good." Prime Minister Jim Bolger summed it up best: "Mission accomplished!"

*P*eter Blake waves to the crowd as the Team New Zealand syndicate director and skipper Russell Coutts are showered with confetti from the crush of well-wishers lining the motorcade route. "There can't be many days much better than this," said Blake. New Zealand's national sporting color—black—shared the spotlight with countless pairs of Peter Blake's lucky red socks.

The celebration culminated (below) with the America's Cup being placed in its new home—the Royal New Zealand Yacht Squadron.

FOLLOWING PAGES:

Black Magic *skipper Russell Coutts offers a "thumbs up" as Auckland celebrates.*

ROUND-ROBIN I
JANUARY 14 - JANUARY 22
Points per win: 1

DAY 1
RACE 1 *Black Magic* def *Rioja de España* by 10:13
RACE 2 *Sydney 95* def *France 2* by 0:20
RACE 3 *Nippon* def *oneAustralia* by 1:06
Day 2
RACE 1 *Black Magic* def *France 2* by 2:40
RACE 2 *Sydney 95* def *Rioja de España* by 3:43
RACE 3 *NZL-39* def *Nippon* by 0:57
Day 3
RACE 1 *oneAustralia* def *Sydney 95* by 3:42
RACE 2 *Black Magic* def *NZL-39* by 4:42
RACE 3 *Nippon* def *France 2* by 0:57
Day 4
RACE 1 *Black Magic* def *oneAustralia* by 1:36
RACE 2 *NZL-39* def *Sydney 95* by 1:24
RACE 3 *Nippon* def *Rioja de España* by 4:03
Day 5
RACE 1 *NZL-39* def *France 2* by 1:32
RACE 2 *oneAustralia* def *Rioja de España* by 1:25
RACE 3 *Black Magic* def *Nippon* by 1:00
Day 6
RACE 1 *oneAustralia* def *France 2* by 1:24
RACE 2 *Nippon* def *Sydney 95* by 4:09
RACE 3 *NZL-39* def *Rioja de España* by 7:03
Day 7
RACE 1 *Black Magic* def *Sydney 95* by WTHD
RACE 2 *France 2* def *Rioja de España* by 3:42
RACE 3 *NZL-39* def *oneAustralia* by 3:52

FIRST ROUND STANDINGS

BOAT	W	L	Points
Black Magic	6	0	6
NZL-39	5	1	5
Nippon	4	2	4
oneAustralia	3	3	3
Sydney 95	2	4	2
France 2	1	5	1
Rioja de España	0	6	0

ROUND-ROBIN II
JANUARY 29 - FEBRUARY 7
Points per win: 2

DAY 1
RACE 1 *Nippon* def *Rioja de España* by 1:48
RACE 2 *Black Magic* def *Sydney 95* by 1:56
RACE 3 *oneAustralia* def *NZL-39* by 1:07
Day 2
RACE 1 *oneAustralia* def *France 3* by 1:27
RACE 2 *Black Magic* def *Nippon* by 0:12
RACE 3 *Sydney 95* def *Rioja de España* by 2:14
Day 3
RACE 1 *NZL-39* def *Sydney 95* by 12:24
RACE 2 *oneAustralia* def *Black Magic* by DSQ
RACE 3 *France 3* def *Nippon* by 2:24
Day 4
RACE 1 *France 3* def *Sydney 95* by 6:49
RACE 2 *NZL-39* def *Nippon* by 1:47
RACE 3 *oneAustralia* def *Rioja de España* by 4:13
Day 5
RACE 1 *Black Magic* def *France 3* by 1:16
RACE 2 *NZL-39* def *Rioja de España* by 15:04
RACE 3 *Nippon* def *oneAustralia* by DNF
Day 6
RACE 1 *Black Magic* def *NZL-39* by 0:54
RACE 2 *France 3* def *Rioja de España* by 0:22
RACE 3 *oneAustralia* def *Sydney 95* by 0:19
Day 7
RACE 1 *Nippon* def *Sydney 95* by 32:03
RACE 2 *NZL-39* def *France 3* by 3:00
RACE 3 *Black Magic* def *Rioja de España* by 20:50

SECOND ROUND STANDINGS

BOAT	ROUND		OVERALL		
	W	L	W	L	Points
Black Magic	5	1	11	1	16
NZL-39	4	2	9	3	13
oneAustralia	5	1	8	4	13
Nippon	3	3	7	5	10
France 3	3	3	4	8	7
Sydney 95	1	5	3	9	4
Rioja de España	0	6	0	12	0

ROUND-ROBIN III
FEBRUARY 15 - FEBRUARY 23
Points per win: 4

DAY 1
RACE 1 *Sydney 95* def *France 3* by 0:38
RACE 2 *Black Magic* def *Nippon* by 1:34
RACE 3 *NZL-39* def *Rioja de España* by 2:30
Day 2
RACE 1 *Black Magic* def *France 3* by 1:39
RACE 2 *oneAustralia* def *Rioja de España* by 4:00
RACE 3 *Nippon* def *Sydney 95* by 2:45
Day 3
RACE 1 *oneAustralia* def *France 3* by 1:05
RACE 2 *NZL-39* def *Nippon* by 7:34
RACE 3 *Black Magic* def *Rioja de España* by 6:59
Day 4
RACE 1 *oneAustralia* def *Nippon* by 8:40
RACE 2 *Rioja de España* def *Sydney 95* by 11:26
RACE 3 *NZL-39* def *France 3* by 6:23
Day 5
RACE 1 *Black Magic* def *oneAustralia* by 0:26
RACE 2 *France 3* def *Rioja de España* by 6:56
RACE 3 *NZL-39* def *Sydney 95* by 4:07
Day 6
RACE 1 *oneAustralia* def *Sydney 95* by 1:59
RACE 2 *Black Magic* def *NZL-39* by 1:28
RACE 3 *Nippon* def *Rioja de España* by 1:51
Day 7
RACE 1 *Black Magic* def *Sydney 95* by 3:18
RACE 2 *France 3* def *Nippon* by 2:17
RACE 3 *oneAustralia* def *NZL-39* by 3:00

THIRD ROUND STANDINGS

BOAT	ROUND		OVERALL		
	W	L	W	L	Points
Black Magic	6	0	17	1	40
oneAustralia	5	1	13	5	33
NZL-39	4	2	13	5	29
Nippon	2	4	9	9	18
France 3	2	4	6	12	15
Sydney 95	1	5	4	14	8
Rioja de España	1	5	1	17	4

ROUND-ROBIN IV
MARCH 2 - MARCH 8
Points per win: 5

DAY 1
RACE 1   *Black Magic* def *France 3* by 2:42
RACE 2   *NZL-39* def *Nippon* by 0:41
RACE 3   *oneAustralia* def *Rioja de España* by DNS

DAY 2
RACE 1   *Black Magic* def *Sydney 95* by 3:24
RACE 2   *oneAustralia* def *Nippon* by 4:44
RACE 3   *NZL-39* def *Rioja de España* by 1:22

DAY 3
RACE 1   *Rioja de España* def *Sydney 95* by 1:15
RACE 2   *Black Magic* def *NZL-39* by 2:35
RACE 3   *Nippon* def *France 3* by 3:38

DAY 4
RACE 1   *Sydney 95* def *Nippon* by 1:22
RACE 2   *Rioja de España* def *France 3* by DNF
RACE 3   *Black Magic* vs. *oneAustralia*, NO RESULT

DAY 5
RACE 1   *NZL-39* def *Sydney 95* by 5:50
RACE 2   *Black Magic* def *Rioja de España* by 1:15
RACE 3   *France 3* def *oneAustralia*, DNS

DAY 6
RACE 1   *NZL-39* def *France 3* by 2:38
RACE 2   *Black Magic* def *Nippon* by 0:57
RACE 3   *oneAustralia* def *Sydney 95* by 1:54

DAY 7
RACE 1   *oneAustralia* def *NZL-39* by 0:57
RACE 2   *France 3* def *Sydney 95* by 0:57
RACE 3   *Nippon* def *Rioja de España* by 0:13

FINAL ROUND-ROBIN STANDINGS

BOAT	ROUND W	L	OVERALL W	L	Points
Black Magic	5	0	22	1	65
oneAustralia	4	1	17	6	53
NZL-39	4	2	17	7	49
Nippon	2	4	11	13	28
France 3	2	4	8	16	25
Rioja de España	2	4	3	21	14
Sydney 95	1	5	5	19	13

SEMIFINALS
MARCH 18 - MARCH 31

DAY 1
RACE 1   *oneAustralia* def *Nippon* by 2:39
RACE 2   *Black Magic* def *NZL-39* by 2:15

DAY 2
RACE 1   *NZL-39* def *oneAustralia* by 1:19
RACE 2   *Black Magic* def *Nippon* by 6:14

DAY 3
RACE 1   *NZL-39* def *Nippon* by 0:57
RACE 2   *Black Magic* def *oneAustralia* by 0:39

DAY 4
RACE 1   *NZL-39* def *Nippon* by 0:23
RACE 2   *Black Magic* def *oneAustralia* by 2:29

DAY 5
RACE 1   *oneAustralia* def *Nippon* by 1:39
RACE 2   *Black Magic* def *NZL-39* by 1:44

DAY 6
RACE 1   *oneAustralia* def *NZL-39* by 0:40
RACE 2   *Black Magic* def *Nippon* by 3:54

DAY 7
RACE 1   *oneAustralia* def *Nippon* by 1:10
RACE 2   *Black Magic* def *NZL-39* by 1:28

DAY 8
RACE 1   *oneAustralia* def *NZL-39* by 1:43
RACE 2   *Black Magic* def *Nippon* by 3:45

DAY 9
RACE 1   *NZL-39* def *Nippon* by 2:26
RACE 2   *Black Magic* def *oneAustralia* by 2:39

DAY 10
RACE 1   *NZL-39* def *Nippon* by 0:55
RACE 2   *oneAustralia* def *Black Magic* by DNS

DAY 11
RACE 1   *oneAustralia* def *Nippon* by 2:41
RACE 2   *NZL-39* def *Black Magic* by DNS

SEMIFINAL STANDINGS

BOAT	W	L
Black Magic	9	2
oneAustralia	7	4
NZL-39	6	5
Nippon	0	11

LOUIS VUITTON CUP FINALS
APRIL 11 - APRIL 21
Best 5-of-9

APRIL 11
RACE 1   *Black Magic* def *oneAustralia* by 4:55

APRIL 13
RACE 2   *Black Magic* def *oneAustralia* by 1:57

APRIL 14
RACE 3   *Black Magic* def *oneAustralia* by 2:26

APRIL 15
RACE 4   *oneAustralia* def *Black Magic* by 0:15

APRIL 17
RACE 5   *Black Magic* def *oneAustralia* by 3:54

APRIL 20
RACE 6   *Black Magic* def *oneAustralia* by 2:13

***Black Magic* wins the Louis Vuitton Cup, 5-1**

ABBREVIATIONS:
DNS: Did not start
DNF: Did not finish
DSQ: Disqualified via protest decision
WTHD: Withdrew voluntarily
NO RESULT: Leader Black Magic *withdrew from race after* oneAustralia *sank (March 5, 1995).*

THE CITIZEN CUP • DEFENDER RACES FOR THE AMERICA'S CUP

ROUND-ROBIN I
JANUARY 13 - JANUARY 22
Points per win: 1

RACE 1   *America³ def Stars & Stripes by 1:16*
RACE 2   *Stars & Stripes def America³ by 5:47*
RACE 3   *Young America def America³ by 0:37*
RACE 4   *Young America def America³ by 3:32*
RACE 5   *Young America def Stars & Stripes by 0:18*
RACE 6   *Young America def Stars & Stripes by 5:00*
RACE 7   *Young America def America³ by 2:02*
RACE 8   *Stars & Stripes def America³ by 1:51*
RACE 9   *Stars & Stripes def America³ by 3:09*

FIRST ROUND STANDINGS

BOAT	W	L	Points
Young America	5	1	5
Stars & Stripes	3	3	3
America³	1	5	1

ROUND-ROBIN II
JANUARY 29 - FEBRUARY 7
Points per win: 2

RACE 1   *America³ def Young America by 0:14*
RACE 2   *Stars & Stripes def Young America by WTHD*
RACE 3   *Stars & Stripes def America³ by 1:29*
RACE 4   *Stars & Stripes def America³ by 4:45*
RACE 5   *Young America def Stars & Stripes by 1:46*
RACE 6   *Stars & Stripes def America³ by 0:28*
RACE 7   *Young America def America³ by 3:02*

SECOND ROUND STANDINGS

BOAT	ROUND		OVERALL		
	W	L	W	L	Points
Young America	2	2	7	3	9
Stars & Stripes	3	1	6	4	9
America³	1	3	2	8	2

Note: Not all races were scored in the second round due to weather-related failure to complete the second set of races in this round.

ABBREVIATIONS:

ABAN: Race abandoned before finish due to time limit expiring.
DNF: Did not finish
WTHD: Losing boat withdrew due to equipment failure.

ROUND-ROBIN III
FEBRUARY 15 - FEBRUARY 24
Points per win: 4

RACE 1   *America³ def Stars & Stripes by 1:26*
RACE 2   *Young America def America³ by 1:20*
RACE 3   *Stars & Stripes def America³ by 1:08*
RACE 4   *Young America def Stars & Stripes by 8:35*
RACE 5   *Young America def America³ by 2:24*
RACE 6   *Stars & Stripes def Young America by 0:03*
RACE 7   *Stars & Stripes def Young America by 1:33*
RACE 8   *Young America def America³ by 1:19*
RACE 9   *Stars & Stripes def America³ by 1:52*

THIRD ROUND STANDINGS

BOAT	ROUND		OVERALL		
	W	L	W	L	Points
Young America	4	2	11	5	25
Stars & Stripes	4	2	10	6	25
America³	1	5	3	13	7

ROUND-ROBIN IV
MARCH 2 - MARCH 10
Points per win: 7

RACE 1   *Stars & Stripes def Mighty Mary by 0:23*
RACE 2   *Mighty Mary def Young America by 0:56*
RACE 3   *Young America def Stars & Stripes by 1:03*
RACE 4   *Mighty Mary def Stars & Stripes by DNF*
RACE 5   *Young America def Mighty Mary by 4:35*
RACE 6   *Young America def Stars & Stripes by 2:06*
RACE 7   *Stars & Stripes def Mighty Mary by 1:35*
RACE 8   *Young America vs. Mighty Mary, ABAN*

FINAL ROUND-ROBIN STANDINGS

BOAT	ROUND		OVERALL		
	W	L	L	L	Points
Young America ˣ	3	1	14	6	46
Stars & Stripes ʸ	1	3	11	9	32
Mighty Mary	2	2	5	15	21

Note 1: Not all races were scored in the fourth round due to weather-related failure to complete the second set of races in this round. Note 2: America³ syndicate substituted Mighty Mary for America³ in round-robin IV. x: Earned two bonus wins in semifinals for winning round-robin series. y: Earned one bonus win in semifinals for placing second in round-robin series.

SEMIFINALS
MARCH 18 - APRIL 3

RACE 1   *Young America def Mighty Mary by 0:32*
RACE 2   *Mighty Mary def Stars & Stripes by 1:36*
RACE 3   *Young America def Stars & Stripes by 0:28*
RACE 4   *Stars & Stripes def Mighty Mary by DNF*
RACE 5   *Young America def Mighty Mary by 0:47*
RACE 6   *Young America def Stars & Stripes by DNF*
RACE 7   *Mighty Mary def Young America by 0:38*
RACE 8   *Stars & Stripes ᶻ vs. Mighty Mary, NO CONTEST*
RACE 9   *Young America def Mighty Mary by 1:44*
RACE 10   *Young America def Stars & Stripes by 0:44*
RACE 11   *Mighty Mary def Stars & Stripes by 2:04*
RACE 12   *Young America def Stars & Stripes by 0:52*
RACE 13   *Stars & Stripes def Mighty Mary by 4:49*
RACE 14   *Mighty Mary def Stars & Stripes by 5:59*

SEMIFINAL STANDINGS

BOAT	W	L
Young America ˣ	9	1
Mighty Mary ʸ	4	5
Stars & Stripes	3	7

x: Earned two bonus wins in finals for winning semifinals.
y: Earned one bonus win in finals for placing second in semifinals.
z: Stars & Stripes won by 1:31, but race was thrown out by international jury because Stars & Stripes sailed with illegal modification.

CITIZEN CUP FINALS
APRIL 10 - APRIL 26

RACE 1   *Mighty Mary def Young America by 0:48*
RACE 2   *Stars & Stripes def Young America by 1:15*
RACE 3   *Stars & Stripes vs. Mighty Mary, ABAN*
RACE 4   *Stars & Stripes def Mighty Mary by 2:50*
RACE 5   *Young America def Mighty Mary by 1:24*
RACE 6   *Stars & Stripes def Young America by 0:01*
RACE 7   *Mighty Mary def Stars & Stripes by 0:41*
RACE 8   *Young America def Mighty Mary by 2:46*
RACE 9   *Stars & Stripes def Young America by 0:45*
RACE 10   *Stars & Stripes def Mighty Mary by 1:02*
RACE 11   *Mighty Mary def Young America by 1:08*
RACE 12   *Young America def Stars & Stripes by 0:52*
RACE 13   *Stars & Stripes def Mighty Mary by 0:52*

FINAL STANDINGS

BOAT	W	L
Stars & Stripes	6	2
Young America	5	5
Mighty Mary	4	5

Stars & Stripes wins the right to defend the America's Cup

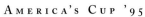

MAY 6 - MAY 13

RACE 1   *Black Magic* def Team Stars & Stripes by 2:45

RACE 2   *Black Magic* def Team Stars & Stripes by 4:14

RACE 3   *Black Magic* def Team Stars & Stripes by 1:51

RACE 4   *Black Magic* def Team Stars & Stripes by 3:37

RACE 5   *Black Magic* def Team Stars & Stripes by 1:50

Black Magic wins the America's Cup

The Royal New Zealand Yacht Squadron in Auckland, New Zealand, will host the next America's Cup.

YEAR	DEFENDER	NATION	CHALLENGER	NATION	WINNER	SCORE
1851*	15 British Yachts	England	America	USA	America	1-0
1870	Magic	USA	Cambria	England	Magic	1-0
1871	Columbia/Sappho	USA	Livonia	England	Columbia/Sappho	4-1
1876	Madeleine	USA	Countess of Dufferin	Canada	Madeleine	2-0
1881	Mischief	USA	Atalanta	Canada	Mischief	2-0
1885	Puritan	USA	Genesta	England	Puritan	2-0
1886	Mayflower	USA	Galatea	England	Mayflower	2-0
1887	Volunteer	USA	Thistle	Scotland	Volunteer	2-0
1893	Vigilant	USA	Valkyrie II	England	Vigilant	3-0
1895	Defender	USA	Valkyrie III	England	Defender	3-0
1899	Columbia	USA	Shamrock	England	Columbia	3-0
1901	Columbia	USA	Shamrock II	England	Columbia	3-0
1903	Reliance	USA	Shamrock III	England	Reliance	3-0
1920	Resolute	USA	Shamrock IV	England	Resolute	3-2
1930	Enterprise	USA	Shamrock V	England	Enterprise	4-0
1934	Rainbow	USA	Endeavour	England	Rainbow	4-2
1937	Ranger	USA	Endeavour II	England	Ranger	4-0
1958	Columbia	USA	Sceptre	England	Columbia	4-0
1962	Weatherly	USA	Gretel	Australia	Weatherly	4-1
1964	Constellation	USA	Sovereign	England	Constellation	4-0
1967	Intrepid	USA	Dame Pattie	Australia	Intrepid	4-0
1970	Intrepid	USA	Gretel II	Australia	Intrepid	4-1
1974	Courageous	USA	Southern Cross	Australia	Courageous	4-0
1977	Courageous	USA	Australia	Australia	Courageous	4-0
1980	Freedom	USA	Australia	Australia	Freedom	4-0
1983	Liberty	USA	Australia II	Australia	Australia II	4-3
1987	Kookaburra III	Australia	Stars & Stripes	USA	Stars & Stripes	4-0
1988	Stars & Stripes	USA	New Zealand	New Zealand	Stars & Stripes	2-0
1992	America³	USA	Il Moro di Venezia	Italy	America³	4-1
1995	Young America	USA	Black Magic	New Zealand	Black Magic	5-0

* Originally named the Hundred Guinea Cup, the America's Cup derived its name from the yacht that first won the Cup in 1851.

STAFF AND ORGANIZATION

SAN DIEGO YACHT CLUB — TRUSTEE

BOARD OF DIRECTORS
Commodore Michael A. Morton
Vice Commodore William Munster
Rear Commodore Richard W. Virgilio, M.D.
John Driscoll
John Pedlow
Ralph Richey
Robert Spriggs
J. Frank Thompson
Tom Fetter, Jr., Staff Commodore

AMERICA'S CUP '95

BOARD OF DIRECTORS
Chairman Frank L. Hope
Leslie L. "Pete" Case
Arthur DeFever
J. Gerald Driscoll, III
Frederick A. Frye, M.D.
Gail Stoorza-Gill
Richard B. Gulley
Morgan Dean Oliver
H. P. "Sandy" Purdon

MANAGEMENT
Charles L. Nichols, *President*
G. Wytie Cable, *Executive Vice President*
Christopher G. Capen, *Director of Marketing and Sponsorship*
Sharon Cloward, *Administrative Assistant*
Lori Graff, *Manager of Accounting, Personnel Administrator*
Carol Ann Henderson, *Manager of Sponsor Relations*
John Pedlow, *Crowd Control Manager*
Anne Sandison, *Director of Community/ Media Relations and Special Events*
Troy Sears, *Assistant to the President*
Jim Shillito, *Chief Financial Officer*

ACTV
(Courtesy of Louis Vuitton)
PAGES: 70-A, 70-B, 70-C

Mathew Antanian
PAGE: 77

Carlo Borlengi
PAGES: 49, 159

Craig Davis
PAGE: 104

Bob Grieser
PAGES: 12-B, 12-C, 13, 15, 26, 28, 29, 32, 34-B, 35-C, 35-F, 35-E, 35-B, 35-A, 35-D, 37-A, 37-B, 38, 39, 41, 42, 44, 45, 46, 47, 48, 50-A, 50-B, 52, 53-A, 53-B, 54-A, 54-B, 55, 56, 59, 60-A, 60-B, 64, 68, 74, 75, 76, 78, 79-A, 79-B, 83, 85, 86, 88-89, 90, 91, 108, 109, 110-A, 111, 115-A, 115-B, 116, 117, 119, 123, 124, 125, 126-127, 128, 134, 135, 136, 137, 138, 139, 143, 144, 145, 146, 147, 151, 156

Kevin Halle
PAGE: 33

Barbara Martin
PAGES: 67, 71, 80-81

Mystic Seaport Museum, Inc.
PAGE: 17

Martin Raget
PAGES: 84-A, 84-B

Rosenfeld Collection, Mystic Seaport Museum, Inc., James Burton Photographer
PAGES: 21-A, 21-B, 22

Rosenfeld Collection, Mystic Seaport Museum, Inc.
PAGES: 23, 24-A, 24-B, 25, 27

Sally Samins
PAGES: 4-5, 8, 30, 31, 40, 58, 66, 69, 72-73, 87, 92, 93, 94-95, 98, 99, 100, 101, 110-B, 112-113, 114, 118, 120-121, 129, 130, 131, 140-141, 148-149, 152

San Diego Yacht Club
PAGES: 12-A, 61

David Shuler
PAGES: 57, 62-63

Kaoru Soehata
PAGES: 1, 2-3, 6-7, 36, 43, 51, 82, 96, 97, 102-103, 105, 106, 107, 122, 132-133, 142, 150, 153, 154-155, 158, 160, 161, 162-163

Mary Anne Stets, Mystic Seaport Museum, Inc.
PAGES: 14, 16, 18, 19

Claire White-Peterson, Mystic Seaport Museum, Inc.
PAGE: 20